5/13/2013

snacks

snacks

Adventures in Food, Aisle *by* Aisle

marcy smothers

HarperOne
An Imprint of HarperCollinsPublishers

HarperOne

HarperCollins books may be purchased for educational, business, or sales promotional use. For information, please e-mail the Special Markets Department at SPsales@harpercollins.com.

HarperCollins website: http://www.harpercollins.com

HarperCollins®, ■®, and HarperOne™ are trademarks of HarperCollins Publishers.

FIRST EDITION

Designed by Campana Design

Illustrations by Sheryl Chapman

Library of Congress Cataloging-in-Publication Data is available upon request.

ISBN 978–0–06–213074–7

13 14 15 16 17 RRD(c) 10 9 8 7 6 5 4 3 2 1

For Germy and Fa

contents

foreword

Ever since I was a little kid in the way-up northern California town of Ferndale, I've been the guy who always had something to say . . . no matter what the subject matter. Whether it's how to hitch a trailer or how to make the perfect spaghetti carbonara. I like to think I know a lot about a lot, and I'm definitely not shy to let people know. It's no secret that I got it from my dad, Jim, who's got something to say on just about every topic. He knows his stuff and, well, I like to think I do too. So for my entire life, I've been spitting out advice and everyday truths to people . . . some wanted, some not so much. But at the end of the day, I think I've got things to say and I appreciate people listening . . . at least most of the time.

And as you might guess, there's no subject matter that fires me up more than food. It's important. It's everything to us. It's the common thread that unites us all. And next to my family, there's nothing I care about more than food and cooking. So I've been known to spit some serious knowledge on the topic to just about anyone who will listen.

When my business partner and I first opened Johnny Garlic's in Santa Rosa in 1996, I was a one-man marketing machine. We were truly bootstrapping it, and we didn't have the luxury of a big marketing and PR budget. Actually, we didn't have a budget at all. So in the very beginning, I'd beg, borrow, and steal to get a little extra mojo for my little restaurant. Luckily, we were right next door to the local radio station, so I'd run over and bribe the DJs to get some airtime. I'd stuff them full of Cajun Chicken Alfredo until they cut me off of the mic, and it was a win-win for us both. Over that time, I really learned to love the radio as a medium, as a voice, and for what it could do for my business. . . . I seemed to have a knack for it too. Of course, I had no idea what would happen a handful of years later.

Cut to about ten years later and I've been pushed into this Food Network competition called the *Food Network Star*. While I didn't want to try out, my buddy Mustard finally talked me into it, and low and behold, I made the finals. Well, at this point, it's go-big-or-go-home time, so I decided to get the word out to get the win . . . and I went straight to the radio. It was my time to really blow it up . . . to talk some smack . . . show my skills . . . spout off some of my knowledge on food and cooking. And here comes Marcy Smothers. *Wow.* What a spitfire. She's spouting her SNACKS in my face from the moment we hit the air. Smacking me down on everything from my vocabulary to my food knowledge. And I loved every minute of it. We clicked immediately, and when the opportunity arose, we jumped right into a show together, and I've got to say, it was one of the most rewarding experiences I've ever had. I still hope that someday we can pick it up together again, but to be honest, she's doing more than fine without me.

All my krew have nicknames, and Marcy is no exception. I call her "Marcinator" because she is part woman and part machine. I've never seen her in a situation she can't handle. She's in it to win it, no matter what she does. I don't know anyone else that can take a plot of dirt at Sonoma Raceway, trick it out for the NASCAR race with Astroturf, plasma TVs, and an outdoor kitchen, then recite drivers' statistics while pouring wine for her guests. She's the real deal. It's no surprise to me that she knocked it out of the ballpark with her first book.

When Marcy talks about food, I listen. Her passion for knowledge and sharing is not only enriching, it's highly entertaining. She may not let you get a word in edgewise, but what she has to say about food is definitely worth absorbing. She's a natural storyteller, and it really comes across in this book.

When it comes to food and cooking, there are a lot of tidbits of information, or what Marcy calls SNACKS, that are old wives' tales. Or incomplete truths. Or straight-up untruths. But when Marcy gives you the 411, you can bet it's right on the money.

She researches and explores constantly—she just can't get enough. A couple times a month we go hiking with our friends in Sonoma County, and from the moment we step out of the truck until the final descent, she's sharing her foodie-isms, and I've got to say, I can't get enough either.

I've written three cookbooks now and read about a thousand others. It's not so easy to find a new and unique take on the world of food and cooking, but if I can personally make but one suggestion to you, do yourself a favor and read Marcy's *SNACKS.* . . . Your kitchen will be all the better for it.

Love, Peace & Taco Grease,

Guy

introduction

The Snacks Story

Others may be able to let people get away with calling red meat sauce Bolognese, but not me. I'm compelled to explain that in MarcyTown a Bolognese sauce is not red, but a pale pinkish brown, more accurately called a ragu, and uses a small amount of tomato paste, not tomato sauce.

It may border on annoying, but I am someone who tells people everything I know. I love to eat, I love to cook, I love to read, and I love to share what I have learned. My best friend, Nancy, casually explains to those not previously subjected to my rapid-fire fun facts, "That's just Marcy. She does this to us all the time."

Could you stand by silently in the produce aisle if an unsuspecting shopper was pulling a leaf from the crown of a pineapple? Not me. Ripeness can't be determined that way—that's not reliable. It is not unsolicited advice if it's helpful advice, right?

When I was growing up, my mother didn't cook, and my parents went out to eat often by themselves. It was probably because of my fatigue with frozen dinners that I started cooking for myself when I was twelve. At first it was simple things like hamburger patties with Lawry's garlic salt and Tater Tots®. By the time I was fourteen, I made a decent chicken parmesan. It was about this time that I set the kitchen on fire while I was pan-frying a steak. It's still a family joke, because I did as instructed by my parents in an emergency. I walked calmly and slowly upstairs to tell them. It didn't occur to me to turn off the burner before I reported the mishap. Needless to say, the flames leaped from the pan to the cabinets. I was issued the worst possible punishment: grounded for a month—from cooking.

My fond food memories come from my grandmother. She considered cooking a chore, yet she always had dinner on the table precisely at 6:00 P.M. Her fare was uncomplicated and simple: one protein (usually broiled chicken), one starch (sweet potato or rice), one vegetable (broccoli or peas), and always a crisp iceberg salad dressed with Wesson Oil, Regina red wine vinegar, and Salad Supreme. I can't tell you what a luxury it was to have a meal prepared for me by someone I loved so dearly.

As much as I have always enjoyed food, I've had a complicated relationship with it too. In college I was anorexic, obsessively fasting and counting calories. I didn't count just my calories. I counted the calories of anyone who ate with me, and let me tell you, that's not the type of chitchat that gets you asked out on a second date. I really wasn't a candidate for starvation anyway, so I started eating more healthfully, ultimately becoming a *vegetablist*—my term for someone who strives to make veggies 50 percent of their daily diet.

My early career days as a casting assistant were managed on a meager budget. Good food was the number-two priority, just behind rent and always way ahead of spending money on my wardrobe. I may have dressed shabbily, but I ate well. I knew how important food was to me at twenty-four years old, when my dream, nay, hunky boyfriend broke up with me because we were "too different" and I didn't care. He was right. His idea of a great dinner out was cheap steaks at a chain restaurant; mine was sushi, no matter how much I had to scrimp and save for it.

I started seriously cooking after I was married, botching lots of dinners, including a leg of lamb I cooked to well, well, well done and a four-alarm chili that became a ten-alarm chili after I accidentally used cayenne instead of chili powder. To improve my cooking skills, I turned to *The Joy of Cooking*, Marcella Hazan's *Essentials of Classic Italian Cooking*, and *Fine Cooking* magazine.

These days I am still infatuated with food and a bit bossy, living up to my childhood nickname, Bossy Mossy. When I recently suggested to a group of girlfriends that we start our meal with a glass of chardonnay each, split three appetizers, then order a bottle of Pinot Noir to pair with the two mains we'd share, my pal Kitty affectionately dubbed me the Food Traffic Controller. Needless to say, I tend to direct and divert food all the time. Forget the compliment, "You look nice." I prefer, "I'll have what she's having."

I am not a chef, someone who cooks for a living to an exacting standard, nor do I want to be. There are a myriad of reasons—time and training included—but the primary one is that I only like to cook what I like to eat. I am careful to explain that I am a food explorer, not a food expert. I'm an enthusiastic eater and insatiably curious about food.

I've always had a gift for gab, but it wasn't until 2003 that I got paid for it. I received a phone call from the program director of my local radio station in Santa Rosa. Assuming he was asking for an interview with my husband (the funny Smothers Brother), I was about to hand the phone over when he stopped me, "Marcy, I don't want to speak with Tom. I want to speak with you."

He explained that KSRO was looking for fresh talent, interesting people who had a point of view and liked to talk. I liked to talk—at dinner parties—not to thousands of strangers. I couldn't imagine sitting behind a microphone for two hours a day with no experience. Reservations aside, I was coerced into auditioning. I recall stammering and staring at the clock, waiting for the commercials. I talked about NASCAR and my kid's mission project and the merits of Best Foods mayonnaise over Miracle Whip. I was sure I was a bore, yet the program director saw potential and handed me the keys to the studio.

The Marcy Smothers Show aired from 9:00 to 11:00 A.M. Monday through Friday on KSRO in Sonoma County. It was a news talk format that required a tremendous amount of research. I got up at 5:00 A.M. to start scanning the headlines to choose my topics. Deana Kodiak, the morning drive-time traffic reporter, was also my producer. Between fender-bender and highway updates, she e-mailed me stories that I may have missed and booked guests. After I dropped my kids at elementary school at 8:30 A.M., I rushed to the station. By 9:05 I was jabbering about the issues of the day. Most of the shows were not particularly memorable, but there was one show that would change the course of my career.

Guy Fieri, a Santa Rosa restaurant owner, was competing on the second season of *The Next Food Network Star*. Looking for votes, he made the rounds on all the local radio programs, including mine. Our conversation was more like a high-stakes ping-pong match than an interview. He served, and I hit it back. Our on-air chemistry was evident when I admonished Guy to "act his age, not his shoe size," and he thanked me for "throwing him under the bus." It was a spirited debate, replete with chiding and laughter, and after the show we vowed to work with each other again. That spring Guy was crowned the Next Food Network Star, and the rest is television history.

Soon thereafter, seeking a bigger challenge myself, I began filling in on KGO in San Francisco. It was heady stuff sitting in the studio of one of the largest stations in the country. Although I relished the role, I soon discovered that politics, current events, and irate callers weren't for me.

After a brief hiatus, my appetite for radio was ravenous again. One day a colleague casually suggested that I consider a radio program about food and wine. Bingo! That was my bailiwick. I owned a vineyard, and I loved to cook and eat.

I immediately thought of Guy and made the call. Although he was a rapidly rising television star and busy with *Guy's Big Bite,* he agreed to partner with me.

Our first pitch to a major radio station was to KFBK in Sacramento. Explaining our idea for a food and wine lifestyle show, Guy commented, "It will be a corn ucopia of topics."

I interrupted him. "Guy, 'cornucopia' is one word, not two." That led to our classic Lucy and Desi banter. Guy wouldn't back down.

The KFBK executive stopped us, "Is that what your show is all about?"

We were only three minutes into our meeting. I took a deep breath and sheepishly answered, "Yes."

Silence. Lots and lots of silence.

"Well then," he replied, "we'll take it."

Guy's fame, our polar opposite "Beauty and the Beast" personalities, and our shared appreciation for all things culinary became *The Food Guy and Marcy Show.*

We recorded 146 shows at the Kendall-Jackson Wine Center. Our repartee was charged with playfulness, yet we were always serious about the topic on hand. We covered everything from macaroni and cheese to beer bongs, to foie gras, to olive oil. There were a few firsts, oysters for me and a plate full of broccoli for Guy. My dog-eared dictionary was always a subject of ridicule, and I would never let Guy get away with a mispronunciation. On-air teasing aside, we never had a problem attracting top-notch guests.

One day in the midst of all of this, I was nearly tackled by my radio mentor Brent Farris. His station, KZST, carried *The Food Guy and Marcy Show* in the market where Guy and I live, Sonoma County. He handed me a CD and said, "I know how you can promote your show." With a huge grin he went on to explain that I should record a sixty-second *Food Guy and Marcy* radio feature. "You give the feature to the affiliates that carry your show for free, they sell commercials and keep the money, and you get your show plugged on stations across the country. Marcy, you have to do this!"

Guy and I went into the studio with Brent and recorded ten sample spots. I teased listeners with an intriguing question such as, "What do the numbers 128 and 350 have to do with your milk?" The query would keep listeners captive through the sponsor's commercial, and then Guy would give the answer: "There are 128 ounces in a gallon of milk and that requires 350 squirts from the udder of a single dairy cow." By design they were short and sweet and meant to keep the radio audience listening through the commercial break. I called them SNACKS.

A week later I played them for my pal John Lasseter at his home (a good friend who also happens to be an Academy Award–winning director). He was standing behind the kitchen counter and leaned in close to the CD player to hear them. I was nervous.

He began nodding. "These are great. I didn't know how to crack an egg or any of those things. They're so good and interesting, I don't want to hear them just once. SNACKS should be a book, and I'm going to take full credit when it's published."

Man o' Manischewitz. One of the most creative men on the planet is advising me to write a book? What was I going to do?

That question was answered a few months later when Mollie Katzen, iconic cookbook author and Kitchen Cabinet member on *The Food Guy and Marcy Show*, reminisced with me over soba noodles and curried tofu.

"I don't want to impose, but I listened to the SNACKS. They're really good. I think they should be in a book."

I remember looking at her without blinking, as if that would confirm what I heard. I didn't think of myself as a writer. *Mollie was a writer.*

"Like I said, I don't want to step on your toes, but I have an agent I can introduce you to if you're interested," she added.

I still hadn't blinked. "Really?" I gulped.

"Then it's done," Mollie replied in her no nonsense yet motherly style. "I'll take care of it when I get home. Should we order fruit for dessert?"

And so SNACKS went from a simmer to a boil.

Although they were initially conceived as a radio feature—fun food facts packed into bite-size segments—I heeded the advice of John and Mollie and concentrated on writing this book. That way radio listeners wouldn't have to jot down my tips on a burger wrapper while driving. They could read SNACKS at their convenience, just one, or twenty, at a time.

I chose each SNACK just as I chose topics for my radios shows. I figured if I didn't know about something or if something's interesting to me, chances are it will be intriguing to my listeners or readers. SNACKS are my personal "aha" moments combined with my take on familiar culinary themes. Food is the biggest industry in the world and there is a lot to share.

SNACKS is a storybook as much as it is a cookbook. I've included recipes that pair with the SNACKS. That way you can serve an hors d'oeuvre featuring endive and settle the argument about how to correctly pronounce it, too.

If you've ever said to the television, "Potpourri for $1,000, Alex," you're going to feast on *SNACKS*. My SNACKS are riddles and trivia that will keep you guessing and surprise you with the practical answers. Even some of my chef pals have been stumped.

SNACKS are like the proverbial potato chip. You can't have just one.

Come on, have a SNACK!

Aisle One
produce

Should You Sleep with Your Lettuce?

You probably don't want to go nighty-night with your romaine, but you may want to consider using a pillowcase when you store washed lettuce to ensure perfectly crisp lettuce every time.

My grandmother Germy was persnickety about her lettuce. Back in the day there were no prewashed or prepackaged salad mixes; I doubt that she would have used them anyway. She took great pride in meticulously rinsing each leaf and air-drying them on paper towels.

Then she would gently—and I mean gently, because you don't want to bruise the lettuce—place the leaves in a pillowcase. Her pillowcases were always 100 percent cotton. Polyester won't work because it absorbs more water than cotton, and that will lead to a soggy salad.

Finally, Germy would fold the top of the pillowcase and put the lettuce in the refrigerator to rest for several hours. (It can be stored this way for several days.)

When creating a spectacular salad, this technique is just the tip of the iceberg. You're going to seriously thank Germy when you bite into your crisp and crunchy lettuces of love.

What Does Thick Thin and Thin Thick Tell You About Organics?

Thin thick, thick thin, thick thick thin . . . those are the black and white lines that make up the UPC code that is scanned at the market. It includes the price and other information, but the really useful stuff is on the PLU code.

PLU stands for Product Look Up code, and it verifies that the food you are buying is really organic. According to Jeff Cox's *Organic Food Shopper's Guide,* the pesky oval PLU stickers on your produce, the ones you hate because you have to peel them off, can actually help you identify what you are putting in your cart.

Conventional produce has a four-digit code. Organic produce has a five-digit code beginning with a "9."

If you're not sure that the plums costing a dollar a pound more than conventional ones are really organic, be sure there are as many digits on the PLU sticker as there are on one hand.

The Beach Boys Sing About California Girls, I Sing About California Garlic!

Americans consume an average of 4 pounds of garlic a year. Thank goodness Gilroy's Christopher Ranch, the largest California grower of fresh garlic, sells more than 60 million pounds of garlic a year.

California varieties are off-white in color, heart-shaped, and have the brown roots still attached on the bottom of the bulb. If the root is shaved off, the garlic was probably grown in China. Chinese garlic has more water in it, so it tends to be diluted. Flavor is therefore compromised with Chinese garlic, and it's also more difficult to sauté. The big flavor of California garlic means you can use less than you do with Chinese garlic.

When choosing fresh California garlic, the bulbs should be plump and firm. Avoid garlic that is soft, light in weight, or sprouting.

Garlic bulbs should be stored in a cool, dry place. They need ventilation, so do not keep them in a bag or container unless it has holes.

Thin Is Not Always In

If you thought thin was in, you are mis-stalken.

Thin is great when you're trying to squeeze into your jeans, but when it comes to asparagus, the plump stalks usually have more flavor and are less stringy. When selecting your asparagus, look for tips that are completely closed. The stalks tend to be tender as far down as the green extends.

Asparagus doesn't keep long, three days at most. If you don't eat it the day you buy it, store the asparagus upright in several inches of water or wrap the stalks in a wet paper towel and refrigerate.

What Can Your Dog's Toy Teach You About an Artichoke?

They both squeak.

If you hold an artichoke close to your ear and press it gently from both sides, a fresh artichoke will softly squeak. That's because it is well hydrated. Drier artichokes, or those that have been on the shelf a while, don't retain much water and therefore won't squeak.

Now that you've listened to your artichoke, look at it. It should be a healthy green color. If the stem's width is proportionate to the size of the globe, there will be a big heart inside. And by all means, do not discount artichokes that have white blisters or blotches during the winter months. Those are known as "frost kissed" and are coveted for their nutty flavor and tenderness.

Once you get your artichoke home, cut a thin slice off the stem, sprinkle the stem with water, and refrigerate no more than five to seven days before cooking.

Grilled "Rover" Artichokes

Serves 4

One of the best things about food is recalling the first time something special passed over your lips. I ate my first grilled artichoke ten years ago at the Vineyards Inn in Kenwood. It was served as a humble side veggie, but for me it was the star of the plate. I was raised on waterlogged artichokes dipped in cold mayonnaise. This was a revelation! Thank you, Chef Steve Rose, for the inspiration!

2 large artichokes

2 tablespoons soy sauce

1 tablespoon Worcestershire sauce

½ cup olive oil

2 lemons

✤ Trim the artichokes by cutting 2 inches off the top. Snip off the sharp points of the leaves with kitchen scissors. Steam the artichokes until almost done, about 20 to 25 minutes. Remove from heat and immediately place the artichokes in a large bowl of ice water. When cool, place them flat side down on paper towels to drain.

✤ Cut the artichokes in half lengthwise. In the center, remove the fuzzy inner leaves (they are called the choke for a reason) and trim just above the heart line. Place them cut side up in a nonreactive dish (that is a glass or ceramic dish that will not react to acidity). Blend together the soy sauce, Worcestershire, and olive oil and pour it over the artichokes. Marinate them for at least 20 minutes.

✤ Cut the lemons in half and brush the cut sides with olive oil.

✤ Heat the grill to medium-high. Cook the artichokes and lemons on the flat side for 5 minutes. Turn the artichokes over and cook for several more minutes until heated through and caramelized.

✤ Serve each half artichoke with a half lemon. They can be enjoyed hot or at room temperature. Be sure to eat the fleshy bottom part of the leaves only (and of course the heart!).

POSTSCRIPT

Once you've marinated the artichokes, you can keep them in the fridge for two to three days before cooking. These guys are so flavorful you don't need an aioli, but if you're a dipper like me, try dipping the leaves in a spicy mixture of Sriracha, mayo, and lemon, or in a creamy hummus.

Why Should You Sunbathe with Your Spinach?

Sunlight gives our body vitamin D, and it gives spinach its nutrients too.

Plant physiologist Gene Lester of the USDA Agricultural Research Service reports that spinach in clear plastic containers that's exposed to continuous supermarket lights maintains photosynthesis, which helps increase the spinach's vitamins and nutrients even after packaging.

So if you're like me, always reaching for the bag in the back (to get the freshest one), consider taking the one in front, which has been basking in the fluorescents, to gain the extra nutrients.

Do Mushrooms Swim?

Just like fish, mushrooms have gills, but their purpose is to produce spores, not to help mushrooms breathe underwater.

Fish gills are easy to spot, and so are mushroom gills. They are the thin vertical lines underneath the cap of most edible or cultivated mushrooms.

Some recipes call for removal of the gills to make room for stuffing or to prevent the gills from leaching a dark liquid into your dish.

Stuffed-to-the-Gills Mushrooms

30 to 35 servings

I met Jimmy Dean at the Nabisco Dinah Shore golf tournament in the early 1990s. He was colorful, larger than life, and passionate about his namesake product. He gave me a pile of coupons for his sausage, and I've been eating it ever since.

30 to 35 small mushrooms

8 ounces Jimmy Dean Original Sausage

5 ounces goat cheese

6 ounces prepackaged spinach, steamed, drained well, and chopped

¼ cup breadcrumbs, preferably panko

½ cup Parmigiano-Reggiano cheese, finely grated

✛ Preheat the oven to 450°F.

✛ Wash the mushrooms (see "Flour Power," page 122) and remove the stems. Mix the sausage, goat cheese, spinach, and breadcrumbs. Stuff the mixture into the caps. Sprinkle with a generous amount of cheese.

✛ Place mushrooms cap side down on a sheet pan and bake for 20 minutes.

✛ The mushrooms will release water on the bottom of the pan. Lift the mushrooms out with a slotted spatula and place them on a serving platter. Discard the mushroom water.

GLUTEN-FREE AND VEGETARIAN OPTIONS
✛ For a gluten-free option, omit the breadcrumbs.
✛ For a vegetarian version, replace the sausage with chopped mushroom stems.

Would You Put Your Clothes in the Dryer Before the Washer?

Never. Then don't salt your vegetables before you roast them.

Presalting veggies causes them to sweat and steam while they are cooking. The moisture that is released makes it difficult for them to achieve the caramelization and texture you are looking for in dry roasting.

To ensure this effect, don't pack the veggies too tightly together, or they will be just as sweaty as a basketball player in triple overtime.

Salt *after* cooking and just *before* serving to maximize flavor and add a little crunch (I use sea salt or Maldon salt).

You Say En-Dive, I Say On-Deev

I can never decide how to correctly pronounce this sassy chicory with the delightful bitter taste. According to Endive.com, both pronunciations are correct, because there are two different varieties of chicory, and they are each pronounced differently.

Curly endive, which is green and looks like disheveled hippie hair, is pronounced "en-dive." The flatter version with a milder flavor is escarole. Frisée (pronounced "free-zay") is the smallest variety; it is lighter in color and, as the name implies, is frizzy. All of these varieties are grown outdoors.

White or red endive bulbs are pronounced "on-deev." Endive bulbs are not grown outdoors. First, chicory seeds are planted in dirt. The roots are harvested after approximately six months. Next, the chicory roots are put in cold storage for up to ten months, then later "bloomed" in a dark "forcing" room. The absence of exposure to sunlight explains the white and pale colors. The paler the head, the better the flavor.

Endive originated in Belgium, although now it is commercially grown all over the world and always in season. When storing it, wrap the head in a wet paper towel and put it in a plastic bag. It will last in the vegetable drawer of your refrigerator for ten to fourteen days.

Since they never touched soil, endive does not need to be washed. Simply cut off the bottom end and remove any damaged leaves. Remove the inner core if you are serving them raw.

The Proof Is in the Parsley, Not the Pudding

Parsley is traditionally put on the plate to add color or as a garnish or breath freshener. There is yet another purpose for parsley.

As food lore has it, the parsley ritual originated when the chef would place a sprig on the plate to indicate it had passed his inspection. The presence of the parsley assured the waiter that the dish was ready to be served.

Bugs Bunny Was Wrong

When my kids were little, I'd often serve them raw carrots with a meal. I thought I was providing them with the best nutrition. When they asked me to cook the carrots, I always deferred to Bugs Bunny, saying, "He eats them raw. So should you."

I wish I could rewind the clock a few years and start cooking the carrots for my children. More beta-carotene, a powerful antioxidant, is released in cooked carrots than in raw. For every 3.5 ounces of carrots, raw carrots contain 5,800 micrograms of beta-carotene versus boiled, which have 8,000 micrograms.

Before you say, "That's All Folks" to raw carrots for your kids, remember that eating them in any form is far more important than how they are prepared.

Why Did Julia Child Eat Her Salad with Her Fingers?

In the 1920s, the original Caesar salad was invented in Tijuana. Legend has it that Chef Caesar Cardini was scrambling when more customers than anticipated arrived at his restaurant. He had limited ingredients in his kitchen, but he did have romaine lettuce and eggs. Apparently no anchovies (other than small amounts found in Worcestershire sauce), as they are not in the original recipe.

Perhaps it was like a comedian stretching his material, but Cardini made the tossing a tableside show, and the Caesar salad was born.

Cardini used only the hearts of the romaine. The guests were expected to pick up the full leaves to eat the salad. Tearing the lettuce into bite-size pieces was not Cardini's concept.

Julia Child traveled to Cardini's restaurant when she was young. When she re-created the recipe years later, she always recommended eating it traditionally, with your fingers.

If it's good enough for Julia Child, it's good enough for me.

What Can Rice Krispies Teach You About Cooking Mushrooms?

The sound that you hear as you pour milk on Rice Krispies is the same sound you want to hear when you cook mushrooms. Snap, crackle, and pop.

I prefer my mushrooms cooked at a very high heat. The pan should be smoking hot. Add a little bit of oil after the pan is heated (don't use butter, because it will burn). Immediately toss in the mushrooms, but don't crowd the pan, or you'll start steaming the mushrooms, the opposite effect of what we want here. Turn them just a few times and you'll get caramelized mushrooms with fabulous flavors and a crunchy texture.

If you cook mushrooms at a lower temperature, you will be stewing them in their own juices. The good news with this technique is that they can cook a long time and stay soft without becoming mushy.

Don't Let the Tastiest Part of Your Garlic E-Scape

Until recently, the only garlic stalks I was familiar with were the ones braided into a wreath and sold at craft fairs.

Sometimes the stalks, shoots really, are cut off when they're young and green to keep the bulb below from expending energy on them. The long, thin, curling tendrils of hard-neck garlic varieties are known as scapes. They're edible, mighty tasty, and have a delicate flavor less pungent than garlic. Scapes are special, hip, and highly seasonal and can be used differently from garlic. Think of scapes the same way you would scallions or shallots, although they are delicious on their own.

Not all farmers harvest the scapes. If the stalks are left alone and continue to grow, they will eventually straighten out, become tough, and turn the color of the garlic bulb attached to it. That's when they are ready for the aforementioned wreath.

Scapes have a short season, so keep your eyes peeled in the garden and at the farmers' markets during the late spring.

Fresh and Fast

"Fresh" and "fast" aren't two words you'd like used about your teenage daughter. However, when it comes to vegetables, it's a great tip for preparing them.

The fresher the vegetable, the faster it will cook. That's because there is more water in recently harvested vegetables. Older vegetables, or those on the shelf for a while, are drier and will require a longer cooking time.

What Do Green Beans and Poker Have in Common?

Knowing when to fold them.

A perfectly cooked green bean, at least by restaurant standards, will bend when folded, breaking only after the tips have touched each other.

I like my green beans a little bit crunchy; my daughter likes them soft and squeaky.

To end up with green beans just like the pros, fold your green beans and wait for the snap. You'll win the jackpot every time.

Shock Value

I'm not a fan of sudden surprises. However, I do like to shock my veggies.

First I blanch them by cooking the vegetables briefly in boiling water. After they are drained, I immediately "shock" them by placing them briefly in ice water to stop the cooking.

I shock my veggies for three reasons:

1. So I can quickly and easily reheat them just before serving dinner. That leaves me more time to concentrate on last-minute dishes that require more of my attention.

2. To lock in the color. Green vegetables will start to lose their color after cooking 5 to 7 minutes.

3. To store them. On Sundays I will clean, trim, and blanch my veggies so that on busy weeknights they are ready for me to reheat, season, and serve.

Pizza Beans

Serves 8 as a side dish

Germy, my grandmother, was an okay cook. Despite this, she was in charge of family celebratory meals. Germy always served Pizza Beans at Christmas. They were seasonally colorful, I'll give them that, except that all the ingredients were canned. I have updated the recipe to reflect my style of cooking, and although I replaced my grandmother's canned green beans with fresh, I still use canned tomatoes. They are convenient and consistently good.

4 cups green beans, cut into bite-size pieces

1 tablespoon olive oil

3 cloves garlic, thinly sliced

1 (15-ounce) can good-quality diced tomatoes, drained well

¾ teaspoon salt, or to taste

1 cup shredded mozzarella or jack cheese

✤ Place the rack in the upper third of the oven and preheat to 450°F.

✤ Place the beans in boiling salted water and cook until just tender, about 5 to 6 minutes. Drain in a colander and place immediately in an ice-water bath, covering the beans completely. When the green beans are cold, remove them from water and place them on paper towels to dry. You don't want to cook with wet beans, because that dilutes the flavors.

✤ Heat the olive oil in a skillet over medium heat, and then add the garlic. Sauté 2 to 3 minutes, stirring the garlic as it dances. Then add the tomatoes. Simmer 5 minutes. Turn off the heat and mix in the green beans and salt.

✤ Place the bean mixture in a 9 × 9-inch buttered baking dish. Sprinkle shredded cheese on top. Bake for 10 minutes or until cheese is well melted and lightly browned.

✤ When serving family style, be sure you put a trivet on the table under the hot baking dish. You've bean warned.

Undercover Vegetables

Gray broccoli, blue cabbage, black beets? Ick! It's time for veg-ervention!

When cooking vegetables, it's important to understand that acids have an effect on vegetable color pigments. There are some acids you want to trap and others you want to evaporate. It's as simple as boiling water and the decision to use a lid or not.

Green vegetables should be cooked uncovered, so the acids can escape. White and red vegetables should be covered to retain their beneficial acids. Yellow and orange vegetables are less finicky.

No Imitators Allowed

In my world, there is only one reason to have boxed "imitation" mashed potatoes in the pantry, and that's to thicken soups and sauces. Here's the scoop on making real mashed potatoes at home.

Boil potatoes whole with their skins on, especially thin-skinned potatoes like Yukon Golds. The skin acts as a barrier, preventing water from getting into the potato. They are easy to peel after you drain and cool them. If you prefer to cook them peeled, use them immediately or put them briefly in cold water to prevent oxidization until you are ready to use them.

To cook your potatoes evenly, start them in cold water and bring to a boil. Watch your potatoes as they boil, and start testing them before you think they are done. Don't use a fork, because that creates extra entries for water. Use a toothpick or a tool with a single prong. When they are just tender, drain them.

After you have peeled them, chop them in chunks, and return them to the empty pot they were cooked in. Turn the heat on medium-low and keep moving the potatoes around to draw out the extra moisture. Once the potatoes leave a floury film on the pot, you're good to go to the next step.

For me, that's a ricer. I was talked into the contraption at my local culinary store, and I'm still thanking the clerk. The ricer produces a smooth and luxurious consistency. Electric beaters can overwork the potatoes, making them gluey and starchy. You can overdo it by hand too, so be mindful of how much you are mixing.

When it comes to mix-ins—really good butter (room temperature or melted), crème fraîche, sour cream, salt, pepper—that's up to you. No matter what liquid you choose—milk, cream, or buttermilk—be sure it is warm before you add it to the potatoes—that helps to make them creamy.

To keep the mashed potatoes warm until the rest of the meal is ready, put them in a double boiler. If you don't have one, use a stainless steel bowl, cover it with plastic wrap, and set it over a pot of simmering water. If the stovetop is too crowded, covered enamel cast-iron pots, such as Le Creuset, are excellent insulators and can keep your potatoes warm for a few hours on the table or countertop.

It Matters How You Slice It

The more finely you chop or mince your garlic, the more pungent the flavor.

Slicing garlic is the conservative approach, and crushing garlic the most assertive. Smashing garlic or chopping too finely can rupture the garlic's cells, leaving the oil you want to cook with on the cutting board.

If you want to reduce the garlic's sharpness and bite, poach it in milk. Roasting garlic mellows the flavor. One clove of raw garlic is stronger than an entire roasted bulb.

If you buy elephant garlic to go big, go home. It's closer to a leek than garlic and has less of a kick.

Since it is likely you'll have garlic on your hands regardless of how you slice it, rub your hands on a stainless steel sink or steel scouring pad to eliminate odor.

Want to Whittle? Forget the Wood and Get a Carrot

Baby carrots are harvested when they are young, usually about 4 to 5 inches long. What about those little carrots in the cellophane bag? The ones that are only 2 inches long? They may be labeled "baby carrots," but they are actually mature carrots that are pared down into a small shape.

It all started around 1986. Carrot farmer Mike Yurosek, owner of Bunny-Luv, was lamenting the large percentage of carrots deemed unsuitable for retail sale because they were not perfectly formed or were broken. Yurosek figured out how to peel, cut, and whittle down discarded carrots. Those baby, er, mini, carrots became the popular bite-size snack food we know today.

Your Cremini Is All Grown Up

Portobello mushrooms are not an exotic mushroom. They are the fully mature version of the common cremini mushroom.

Portobellos' large, flat, open cap wasn't always considered a gourmet delicacy. According to Sharon Tyler Herbst's *The Food Lover's Companion,* "The name 'portobello' began to be used in the 1980s as a brilliant marketing ploy to popularize an unglamorous mushroom that, more often than not, had to be disposed of because growers couldn't sell them."

Just like wine, portobello mushrooms' flavor changes with age. The flavor of a cremini is light and delicate, and the grown-up portobello tastes thick and meaty.

Going Against the Grain

Onions have a grain just as meat does. Knowing whether to cut with or against the grain can make you a better cook. Both methods have different purposes depending on what you are preparing.

If you slice an onion against the grain, the onion will break up when cooked. That's a good option if you're making a stew or sautéing onions for a steak sandwich.

If you are making something in which you want your onions to hold together while cooking, such as a French onion soup, then slice your onion with the grain. The grain will help keep the onion slices stable as they cook.

Why Should You Take a Bath with Your Strawberries?

Nothing is better than fresh strawberries, and nothing is more disappointing than finding them moldy a day later.

Air-drying them on paper towels and storing them so they don't press against each other is helpful. Putting them in the refrigerator is important, because cold temperatures impede mold growth.

Guess what? Hot water suppresses mold growth too.

Harold McGee studied the effects of hot-water treatments on strawberries. He reported in *The Curious Cook* that if you immerse them in water at 125°F for 30 seconds, you can delay the dreaded moldiness. I tried Mr. McGee's thermotherapy experiment at home. The batch of farm-stand strawberries that I bathed lasted two days longer than those I merely refrigerated.

A bath in water at 125°F is too hot for us mere mortals, but strawberries love it!

Breakfast Berry Brûlée

When my kids were little, I was always looking to supersize the nutritional value of meals anywhere I could. Oatmeal was always a hard sell, but once I made it into a brûlée with strawberries, it was a big hit!

Oatmeal, any unsweetened variety (I prefer McCann's Quick and Easy Steel Cut Irish)

Strawberries, sliced

Blueberries, if desired

Brown sugar

✤ Preheat the oven to broil.

✤ Prepare the oatmeal according to the package directions, depending on how many servings you are making. Place it in a shallow ovenproof bowl or ramekin for an individual serving. For a larger serving, use an 8 × 8-inch dish, but do not use glass, because it's unsafe under the broiler. Lay the berries on top of the oatmeal, covering completely. Sprinkle brown sugar over the berries.

✤ Place the bowls on a sheet pan for easier handling. Cook under the broiler until brown sugar melts and caramelizes. The length of time will vary (usually 3 to 4 minutes), depending on how close the oatmeal is to the broiler. Watch carefully, as this will happen quickly. Burning will happen quickly too, so don't step away from the oven.

✤ You can also achieve a restaurant-perfect result using one of the fancy torches sold at culinary stores.

✤ Serve with care. The dish will be very hot. And delicious.

What Can Romeo and Juliet Teach You About Tomatoes?

Although Juliet was revived, a garden or heirloom tomato, once refrigerated, cannot be.

The aroma of a fresh, ripe tomato is due to the conversion of a chemical called linoleic acid to Z-3 hexenol. Cold interrupts this process. Once a garden tomato goes into the fridge, it can never regain its aroma or original flavor.

The same doesn't hold true for the common grocery-store tomato. Scientists at UC Davis and Cornell University have discovered that the mutation that gives these humdrum tomatoes their uniform appearance and allows them to endure shipping also inadvertently reduces their sugar levels and, ergo, their taste.

Since mass-produced tomatoes have little flavor to begin with, go ahead and put them in the fridge—you can't kill the flavor twice (unlike Juliet).

Going Bananas?

What fruit family do bananas belong to? I'll warn you in advance, it's easy to slip up on this one.

Despite being a tropical fruit, bananas are closer botanically to berries than they are to mangoes.

Bananas are harvested when they are green. They are different from many fruits in that they ripen after they have been picked. If all your bananas ripen at once, you don't have to make banana bread if you're not up for it. Put them in the refrigerator instead. Even though the peel will turn an unsightly brown, the flesh inside will be the familiar white color and fine to eat for several days.

And just to drive you nuts, mangoes are distant relatives of pistachio and cashew trees.

Banana Scallops

About 30 pieces

I inherited a collection of vintage cookbooks, and banana scallops are mentioned in one from 1940. I was intrigued, because bananas cut in 1-inch slices really do look like the mollusks. "Scallop" is also a cooking term that generally means a dish made from slices of food (usually potatoes), with cream or sauce and a crumb or cracker crust on top. Put this all together, and you have a tasty treat that's terrific with caramel sauce and vanilla ice cream.

4 to 5 bananas

12 sugar ice-cream cones

2 eggs

1 tablespoon milk or cream

1 tablespoon vanilla or rum

Vegetable oil for frying

✤ Peel and slice the bananas into 1-inch-thick pieces. Crush the sugar cones in a food processor. Place the crumbs on plate or baking sheet. In a shallow bowl, lightly whip the eggs. Add the milk or cream. Stir in the vanilla or rum. Dip the bananas in the egg mixture, let the excess drip off, and place them in the crumbs, turning to coat. Gently press the crushed sugar cones into all sides of the bananas.

✤ In a fry pan, heat 2 inches of oil on medium-high heat. Fry the bananas in oil briefly, about 1 minute, turning once, until lightly browned. Drain on paper towels.

✤ Serve on a platter or, to really have fun, use small seafood plates shaped like shells.

Arthur Pulled the Sword from the Stone. Can You Pull the Leaf from the Crown of a Pineapple?

You can. But neither ripeness nor quality can be positively determined that way.

The best ripe-o-meter is the presence of fresh (intact) green leaves, a pleasing pineapple aroma at the base, and a fruit that is plump and firm. If the pineapple is yellow all over and soft, reject it. It's probably overripe, and the fruit may be fermented.

If only green pineapples are available, don't assume they are unripe. They may be "green-shell ripe" and purposely grown to be green, not yellow.

Either way, pineapples do not ripen after they are picked. Pineapples should be stored in the refrigerator and will last two to four days.

Cooking with fresh pineapples can be tricky. They contain the enzyme bromelin, which breaks down protein. Be cautious when marinating meat with fresh pineapple or fresh pineapple juice—it can quickly turn from tender to totally tattered. Since the enzyme is destroyed by heat, canned pineapple or pineapple juice is fine to use in marinades.

Good news for Arthur after a long day of dueling with the other knights, bromelin is touted for its anti-inflammatory benefits.

What Do Limes and Lemons Have in Common?

Besides the fact that they are both citrus fruits. That's too easy. The answer is that they are both yellow.

But limes are green!

Yes, limes are green as they are developing. However, when they are fully ripe, their skins are yellow. Just like lemons. This is true for most common varieties in America: Persian, Tahiti, and Bearss.

Limes are tart when green and become sweeter as they age. It's easy to mix up lemons and ripe limes judging by their yellow skins, so I keep them in separate bowls.

Buying Avocados Should Be a Hass-le

There are several varieties of avocado on the market, but my favorite is the creamy Hass. It is commonly misspelled as Haas, but don't be fooled, it is indeed Hass, and the correct pronunciation rhymes with "pass." The Hass variety of avocado is named after postman Rudolph Hass, who patented the fruit in 1935.

Hass avocados are distinctive by their bumpy skin. All avocados ripen after they have been picked, but the skin on Hass avocados changes as they ripen, going from dark green to ready-to-eat purplish black. Color is an indicator, but it's the feel that best predicts how ripe an avocado is. Don't poke it with your finger, as that can bruise the fruit. Instead, put the avocado in the palm of your hand and squeeze gently. It's ready if it yields to the pressure.

If you want two neat halves of avocado for stuffing, don't peel it first. It's easier to remove the skin after it has been halved. Cut the avocado in half, twist the halves gently in opposite directions, and separate. The same method can be used for sliced avocado too. Halve the avocado, remove the pit, make your slices inside the skin, then remove them with a spoon.

If you're in a hurry to get to your guacamole, place an unripe avocado in a brown paper bag with an apple or banana for two to three days at room temperature.

Speaking of guacamole, placing the seed in it helps to prevent browning a bit while it is stored. So does a dash of something acidic like lemon juice or vinegar (which is why a lot of guacamole recipes call for lime juice). But the most important thing is creating a seal by placing plastic wrap directly on top of the guacamole, then storing it in an airtight container in the refrigerator for a few hours.

X Marks the Spot

Peeling tomatoes just got a whole lot easier. How? By making an X-cut, about 1 inch long, on the bottom end.

After the tomato is scored, put it briefly in boiling water. After 30 seconds or so you should see the skin slightly peeling away from the meat. Remove it from the water and plunge it immediately into cold water to cool. Peel the skin off from the X flaps. Cut it in quarters, remove the seeds, and chop as needed for a recipe.

This technique is used for tomato *concasse,* the classic mixture of peeled, seeded, and chopped tomatoes.

The Meat of the Matter

Why are we discussing meat in the produce aisle?

Because fruit has meat.

Why that word? Especially when "meat" is most often defined as the flesh of animals?

"Meat" also means the "chief part." The chief part of the fruit is not the skin, pit, or seeds (with exception of pomegranates)—it's the edible part.

Why Did the Tooth Fairy Visit the Kiwi?

To fetch the tooth, naturally.

Kiwi fruit has a very sharp, tacklike growth just under the root end. It looks similar to a pointed baby tooth. To find it, make a shallow cut at the root end. It will be attached to the core and buried underneath the fruit.

Although I wouldn't suggest leaving the kiwifruit "tooth" under your pillow at night, knowing the drill to pull it out will keep your fruit salad safe.

Do Figs Have Eyes in the Back of Their Heads?

Figs don't have heads, silly, but they do have an eye. It's located on the blossom end.

When it comes to choosing and buying fresh figs, my pal Marie Simmons says it best in her book *Fig Heaven:* "There is an Italian saying, *Il collo d'impiccato e la camicia da furfante,* which means, 'A ripe fig has a neck like a man who has been hanged, and an open shirt like a thief.' In other words, when ripe, the fig stem should be long, narrow, and slightly wrinkled, and the body of the fig should be literally bursting with syrupy sugar."

In less eloquent terms, figs should feel plump and heavy in your hand. They should yield to firm yet gentle pressure. They are highly perishable, so once they are ripe, use them right away. If you need to store them, put them in the refrigerator for a few days tops. Dried figs are far more shelf stable and available all year long.

Figs are fascinating! There is more fiber in one fig than nearly any other fruit or vegetable. Forget the tanning bed. Figs contain psoralen, which is a skin sensitizer that promotes tanning. Want to quit smoking? Figs may help because of their high alkalinity.

Go fig-ure.

Fa's Fig Crostini

About 30 crostini

My grandfather, Fa, was Italian to the core. He adored figs. As a young child, I recall sitting on his lap in the kitchen, eating figs and dripping sticky juice on the plastic kitchen tablecloth. What I miss most about my grandfather is his signature proclamation when he ate something that delighted him, "Oh my God . . ."

Butter, softened for spreading

8 ounces Italian or sourdough baguette, sliced into ½-inch pieces

15 thin slices prosciutto, cut in half

¼ cup fig spread or fig jam (usually found with fine cheese, not jelly)

½ cup ricotta cheese

✤ Preheat oven to 400°F.

✤ Spread the baguette slices with butter. Place them on sheet pan or cookie sheet and lightly toast, 3 to 4 minutes. Spread a layer of fig jam on the toasted baguette slices, followed by a layer of ricotta cheese. Fold the prosciutto to fit the size of the crostini and place it seam side down on the ricotta.

✤ Serve crostini on a warm platter.

Why Do You Need Your Tool Box When Baking Bread?

There are many tricks of the trade when it comes to baking bread. Professional bakery ovens are steam injected. Why? Because steam is one of the secrets to a crispy crust.

How do you re-create that effect in a home oven? With nuts and bolts from your toolbox.

When master baker Michel Suas, founder of the San Francisco Baking Institute, was a guest on *The Food Guy and Marcy Show,* he explained how placing nuts and bolts on the bottom of a heavy skillet or Dutch oven can make a better baguette.

Put a pan with a layer of nuts and bolts on the bottom of the oven and then preheat to the desired temperature. Immediately after placing the bread dough in the oven, pour crushed ice over the hot nuts and bolts in the lower pan. Close the door immediately. Allow your bread to have a steam bath for at least 15 minutes before opening the door. Continue baking as directed by your recipe.

What Traits Do Holes in Your Socks and Holes in Your Bread Share?

Not much. Holes in your socks are a nuisance, but holes in your bread are a blessing.

The size of the holes is partly determined by the amount of water used in the dough (fermentation time plays a big part, too). A dense bread, like a bagel, has far less hydration than a holey bread, like a baguette.

The difference is especially obvious when you compare commercial and artisan loaves. Commercial breads, often made with a lot of yeast and little hydration, tend to be fairly solid. Artisan loaves, which have more hydration and are handled with care, are more likely to have the distinctive feature of an irregular hole structure.

So mend your socks and mind your bread.

The Best Thing Since Sliced Bread

We have Wonder Bread to thank for the pithy aphorism we use to describe something very useful.

Before 1925, bread was only sold in whole loaves, but in that year the Continental Baking Company became the first bakery to introduce presliced bread in America, thus inspiring the saying still popular today, "The best thing since sliced bread."

During World War II, Wonder Bread did its part for the war effort by temporarily stopping production of sliced bread; bread slicers were made of metal and metal was a precious commodity.

Years later Wonder Bread added another innovation. It was one of the first bakeries in the United States to enrich and fortify its white bread with eight essential vitamins and minerals.

Giggle Toasts

24 pieces

I started making these ditties in college. They were quick and inexpensive. Every time someone would ask me for the recipe, I'd list the ingredients, and they would giggle. Was it because they were so easy to make? Or because I used Wonder Bread? Either way, the Wonder Bread is the secret, with its dense and gooey texture, aided by the velvety magic of baked mayonnaise.

6 slices Wonder Bread

8 ounces sharp cheddar cheese, shredded

4 green onions, thinly sliced

½ cup mayonnaise

✤ Set the oven rack in the upper part of the oven, and preheat the oven to broil.

✤ Cut the crusts off the Wonder Bread. Place the whole slices on a foil- or parchment-lined cookie sheet or sheet pan. Mix the grated cheese, green onions, and mayonnaise. Spread the mixture evenly on each slice. Broil until light brown and bubbly.

✤ Cool the toasts just enough to work with them, then cut into fours on the diagonal. Serve immediately and wait for the giggles.

Forget the Da Vinci Code–Break the Bread Code!

Sharing a meal is known as breaking bread, but what about breaking the bread code?

Commercially produced bread that is sold in grocery stores (often) is tagged or twist-tied with a color-coded system that designates which day the bread was baked:

> Monday = Blue
> Tuesday = Green
> Thursday = Red
> Friday = White
> Saturday = Yellow

Can't remember which tag to look for on which day of the week? The colors are alphabetically organized.

POP QUIZ: You are shopping on Wednesday and you want the freshest bread. Which color tag do you look for?

ANSWER: Some commercial bakeries do not bake on Wednesday (or Sunday), so you will need a green tag to ensure your bread is only one day old.

I know that many bakeries stamp the sell-by date on their tags, but that doesn't tell you how old the bread is, and it takes away all the fun!

Why Should You Tell Your Kids to Play with Soldiers at Breakfast?

You may have a house rule to keep toys off the table. However, your kids may be persuaded to finish breakfast if they are served soldiers.

No, not little green army men. Soldiers are a British snack of toast that is traditionally served with a soft-boiled egg. The toast is cut into 1-inch slices and dipped into the runny yolk.

Soldiers are so much fun to eat, your family will salute you.

What Does Lake Erie Know About French Bread?

Boulange and *boulangerie*—are they interchangeable to describe French bakeries?

The answer is in *erie*. A *boulange* sells bread, however usually there is no bakery on the premises. A *boulangerie* is a bakery that also sells bread.

It does not mean that the bread is fresher at the *boulangerie*. The *boulangerie* bakes bread just for the *boulange* and delivers it daily. The only thing missing at the *boulange* is the irresistible baking aroma you'd smell at the *boulangerie*.

Why Did the Miner Sleep with His Bread?

Sourdough bread was ubiquitous during the nineteenth century's Gold Rush. The sourdough starter traveled with the miners from camp to camp. If shelter wasn't available, the camp cook would take the starter to bed with him, as the frigid night air would stop the fermentation.

The miners, prospectors, and pioneers came to be identified by their daily bread and were nicknamed "Sourdoughs."

Kahlua "Mexican" French Toast

I was first introduced to Kahlua in Tijuana on a weekend jaunt with my UCLA pals. The rum-and-coffee based cordial is still my favorite. In this recipe, Kahlua replaces the vanilla. I use sourdough bread, because its sourness contrasts nicely with the Kahlua's sweetness, creating an indulgent adult breakfast.

Serves 4 to 6

3 eggs

2 cups milk

2 tablespoons Kahlua

2 to 3 tablespoons butter (more if needed)

8 slices sourdough bread from round loaf (the various sizes of slices that come from a round loaf suit all appetites)

✚ In a large bowl beat the eggs. Add the milk and Kahlua. Whisk until all the ingredients are combined. Dip each slice of sourdough bread in the egg mixture, lightly coating both sides. (Don't overdo it, or the bread will fall apart.)

✚ Heat a griddle or skillet. Melt enough butter to evenly cover the surface. When it starts to bubble, place 1 or 2 slices of dipped bread on it, without crowding, and cook until each side is well browned.

✚ Serve with room-temperature butter and real maple syrup.

Fumble Fingers and the Cop

That may sound like an old-fashioned Mickey Spillane crime novel, but it's the reason we have French dip sandwiches today.

In 1918, Chef Philippe Mathieu was making beef sandwiches in his Los Angeles restaurant. He accidentally dropped the sliced French roll into the pan holding the meat and all its juices. Mathieu offered his customer, a policeman, a new sandwich with dry bread, but the cop offered to take the sandwich as it was.

The next day the same policeman returned to the restaurant and asked for a "French dip sandwich." And thus the legend and the sandwich were born.

Why the "French"? That's food lore, and even the restaurant, Philippe's Original, which still operates today, doesn't know if it was because Chef Mathieu was French, the bread the sandwich was made on was a French roll, or because the cop's last name was French.

The Split Decision

The history of the English muffin is mired in myth. However, there is one thing that most muffin buffs agree on, and that's the decision to split an English muffin rather than slice it.

Slicing creates a flat surface without much texture. By splitting it with a fork, you create the coarse texture that becomes crispy and crunchy when toasted.

Samuel Bath Thomas knew this, and after he opened his bakery in New York City in 1880, he developed a secret griddle-baking process that produced "nooks and crannies." To ensure the muffins toasted perfectly every time, they were split rather than sliced. "Nooks and crannies" became so easily identified with Thomas' English Muffins, still the number-one bestselling English muffin, that the expression was trademarked. (You may know that a nook is a cozy corner, but did you know that a cranny is a small, narrow space or opening?)

What Do Hot Dog Buns and Washing Machines Have in Common?

They both have the top-loading option.

In New England, hot dog buns are called top-loaders. They are split from top to bottom and have at least one flat side. These top-loading buns are also known as frankfurter rolls or lobster buns.

It is a regional distinction, because everywhere else, hot dog buns are split on the side, just like hamburger buns. They are usually uneven, with more bun on the top than on the bottom.

Frankly, I prefer the top-loaders, because the hot dog and the condiments nestle in so nicely.

The Original Napkin?

The Spartans liked to keep their white togas clean, so how did they wipe their hands and face following a feast?

It was not uncommon for Greeks of that era to use bread as a napkin. Who needs paper napkins when you can have edible ones instead?

What Is a Sponge Doing in Your Bread?

I'm not talking about the yellow rectangle with the scratchy green top, although that is a sponge.

Making a sponge starter for bread will result in better flavor and texture. It differs from the regular yeast method, where yeast is activated with warm water and ferments with the dough in a few hours.

A sponge starter typically uses less yeast than the regular method and ferments longer. When the sponge is ready (usually eight hours to overnight), the rest of the ingredients are added and the dough is kneaded and baked like usual.

Breads made using a sponge starter are tangier and tend to stay moister than breads utilizing the yeastier regular method.

Aisle Three
cheese

What Can a Camel Teach You About Grilled Cheese?

Camels like the Sahara desert, because it is hot and dry. Grilled cheese sandwiches also like a hot and dry environment—the pan.

When my pal Marlena Spieler, author of *Grilled Cheese: Fifty Recipes to Make You Melt*, was a guest on *The Food Guy and Marcy Show*, she emphasized that you should "Brown, not drown, your grilled cheese."

The best technique for a grilled cheese is to put butter onto the bread, not into the pan. Coat the outside of both slices of the bread with soft butter or brush lightly with olive oil.

Any soft cheese will do. Shredded or grated cheese will melt the quickest.

Heat a heavy pan, which will conduct heat most efficiently and produce the coveted crispiness. Nonstick is fine too.

To get over the final hump of a great grilled cheese sandwich, flip and turn it several times, giving it a few good squishes as you go.

Soupwiches

Serves 4 as a main course or 12 as an hors d'oeuvre

One of my favorite comfort foods on a winter night is grilled cheese dipped in tomato soup. The buttery richness of the sandwich and the creamy soup—yum! Here I have a two-for-one special: Tomato soup and grilled cheese in the same sandwich. Mmmm, mmmm good!

½ cup (1 stick) butter, at room temperature

¼ cup Campbell's Tomato Soup, condensed (i.e., straight from the can)

1 tablespoon onion or shallot, minced

8 slices bread (I prefer English muffin bread, if available, or French bread)

2 cups cheddar cheese, shredded

Olive oil

✤ Mix the butter, soup, and onion. Spread 1 tablespoon of tomato-soup butter on each slice of bread. Put ½ cup cheddar cheese on each of four of the slices and close. Press on the Soupwiches to seal. Using a pastry brush, lightly paint the outside of the Soupwiches on both sides with olive oil. Alternately, you can use soft or melted butter.

✤ Heat a heavy or nonstick skillet on medium-high. When it is hot, add Soupwich. Squish and flip a few times until browned on both sides. (You can cook two at a time if your pan is big enough and you can manage twice the squishing and flipping.)

✤ Protect the roofs of your friends' and family's mouths. Cool the Soupwiches for a few minutes. Then cut them in half, plate them, and serve.

✤ If you are serving the Soupwiches as an hors d'oeuvre, remove the crusts and cut into fours on the diagonal.

✤ Go ahead and make the rest of the soup. Be sure to fill the can ¾ full with water, not all the way to the top.

What Can Mike Tyson Tell You About Your Cheese?

Mike Tyson has had bruises that are black, purple, blue, and green.

Molds of the same colors are often found on hard and semihard cheeses. Sometimes the molds are cultivated on purpose, such as *Penicillium roqueforti*, which is used to produce bleu cheese and Roquefort.

If you find those molds growing on hard or semihard cheeses, you can cut off those molds and still enjoy it. Fresh cheeses that have mold must be thrown away.

Pink is a color of healthy skin, but it is not the color of healthy cheese. Most cheese that has developed a pink mold is down for the count and cannot be saved. (Eating it might be riskier than getting into the ring with Mike.)

Give Me a Home Where the Buffalo Roam

I'll admit that I always thought buffalo mozzarella was made in Buffalo, New York, just like the wings.

A few years ago I was visiting Italy and learned that buffalo mozzarella is made from the milk of water buffalos. The buffalo roam in Campania, where their milk is prized for being higher in protein and richer in fat than cow's milk—the perfect ingredient for mozzarella.

Mozzarella comes from the Italian word *mozzarre*, which means "to cut off." The cheese maker starts with a long strand of cheese. Once the mozzarella ball is formed, it is cut off from the rest of the strand and put into a cold brine.

Mozzarella is a fresh cheese and is best consumed as soon as possible after purchase.

Spuntinos

About 30 pieces

Spuntino is the Italian word for "snack." A spuntino can be anything, but since pizza is America's favorite food, I make bite-size pizza-flavored snacks here.

2 sweet Italian sausages, about 6 ounces each, or 12 ounces pepperoni, minced

½ cup pesto, commercial or homemade

6 ounces round wonton wrappers

1 cup mozzarella cheese, shredded

Vegetable oil for frying

Smooshed Sauce (page 141) or prepared red sauce, for dipping

✤ Remove the casings from the sausages, crumble the meat, and cook over medium-high heat. Drain on paper towels and cool. Chop sausage if pieces are larger than a crumble.

✤ Smear pesto sauce on each wrapper, except for the last ¼ inch around the edge. Add a teaspoon of cheese on the bottom half of each circle. Sprinkle sausage or pepperoni on top of the cheese. Do not overload the wrapper. Dip your index finger in cool tap water and run it along the exposed edges. Fold the pesto-only side over on top of the fillings. Seal tightly.

✤ Heat 1 inch of vegetable oil in a fry pan over medium-high heat. When the edge of a spare wrapper is dipped in the oil and it sizzles, it's time to start frying. Cook 2 to 3 at a time, turning once, until lightly golden brown. Drain on paper towels.

✤ Serve with warm red sauce.

POSTSCRIPT
Wrappers usually come in 12-ounce packages. Freeze the other half or double the recipe.

What Do Ab Exercises and a Famous Italian Cheese Have in Common?

The crunch.

The first time I ate a slice of Parmigiano-Reggiano, its grainy texture surprised me. To be honest, I wasn't sure if the crunch was on purpose.

I've since learned that the crystallization in the cheese is a result of the aging process. As the cheese's proteins break down, the amino acids crystallize, and it's the crystals that make the crunch. The longer the cheese ages, the crunchier the cheese becomes. Which is saying something, because Parmigiano-Reggiano ages for an average of twenty-four months, the longest of any hard cheese, before it goes to market.

Is it really worth the extra money to buy authentic imported Parmigiano-Reggiano? Yes! You can tell by the pin dots pressed into the rind. That assures you that the cheese was made under the strict *Consorzio del Formaggio* standards in northern Italy.

Please don't throw away the rind when you're finished with your Parmigiano-Reggiano—use it in your next sauce or soup as an incredible flavor booster. I freeze any I can't use right away.

Not Your Typical Taco Salad

25 to 30 pieces

Taco salad takes on a whole new meaning here. The cheese isn't on the salad; it's molded into a taco shell. These beauties are terrific for a party when your guests are eating on their feet.

SHELLS

2 cups (8 ounces) Parmigiano-Reggiano cheese, shredded

DRESSING

1 tablespoon lemon juice

1 clove garlic, minced

1 teaspoon white wine vinegar

¼ teaspoon Worcestershire sauce

⅓ cup olive oil

¼ teaspoon salt

SALAD

2 cups chopped romaine

2 cups mixed greens

SHELLS

✤ Preheat the oven to 350°F.

✤ Place parchment paper on a sheet pan. Using 3-inch ring mold, place 1 rounded tablespoon of cheese in an even layer inside the ring to form circle. Space them at least 2 inches apart to allow for spreading. If you don't have a ring mold, draw 3-inch circles on the parchment paper with a pencil, then turn the paper over so the pencil lead doesn't transfer onto the food. Use 1 rounded tablespoon of cheese to fill each circle.

✤ Bake 8 to 10 minutes or until light golden brown.

✤ Remove from the oven. Cool 2 to 3 minutes, then fold the cheese circles in half to form a small taco shell. Gently press the center down on the paper to create a flat-bottomed crease, so the shells will stand up on the platter instead of falling on their sides. Fold them all as quickly as possible before they become too stiff to mold.

DRESSING

✤ Whisk all the ingredients together and set aside.

SALAD

✤ Toss the greens with the dressing and fill the taco shells with the salad. Arrange on a platter and serve.

Bad Wrap

Boom chicka boom, chicka boom boom. Now that's a bad rap!

When it comes to storing cheese, it needs a good wrap to remain fresh and flavorful. Cheese likes to be covered, otherwise it will absorb the aromas around it. Wrap it loosely in wax or parchment paper. If all you have is plastic, that's fine, just don't wrap it too tightly because that encourages bacteria and mold growth, plus trace amounts of chemicals from the plastic might infiltrate the cheese.

Every time you use the cheese, wrap the leftovers in new wax or parchment paper. (It's the same idea as changing your sheets.) If you don't, I'll start singing again.

PAC-MAN and Cheese

There is no need to avoid all cheese if you're lactose intolerant.

At least when it comes to aged cheese.

Lactose is the milk sugar that feeds the bacteria that makes the cheese. As the bacteria eats, the lactose is depleted, and in about sixty days the bacteria will have consumed most of the lactose.

Have you ever noticed that arcade-game hero PAC-MAN looks like a yellow wheel of cheese with a wedge removed? It may be a coincidence, but he can help me explain how bacteria eats lactose:

The PAC-MAN screen is full of dots (lactose) on day one of cheese making. PAC-MAN (the bacteria) maneuvers around the cheese and in sixty days the dots (lactose) are gone and you get a new game (lactose-less cheese).

Fresh cheeses such as cottage and cream cheese, and process cheeses like Velveeta (correctly called "process," not "processed"), have the most lactose. Fun facts aside, consult your physician to make sure cheese aged sixty days or more is safe for you.

The Cheese Nanny

Young ones require nurturing and someone to watch over them. Someone who is sensitive to the various stages of development and can assess instantly what care is needed. If you can't do it all yourself, you hire a caregiver.

I'm not talking about a nanny for your kids. I'm talking about a nanny for your cheese.

In France it is not uncommon for a cheese maker to give guardianship of their cheese to an *affineur*, sending their cheese far from where it was made, so that it can be cared for by an expert.

Affineur is a highly respected profession.

Many of the cheese's characteristics are acquired during aging. The affineur finishes the cheese, applying treatments to the rinds, turning the cheese, tapping it, and monitoring temperature and humidity. It is a mystical calling that requires loving attention to detail and that results in divine cheese.

When the aging process is complete, the affineur sends the cheese home, perfectly aged, or packages it, sending it out to the world.

If only the cheese nanny would take our Brie *and* our brats.

Rind and Reason

Rinds are intended to protect the cheese.

The question of whether or not to eat the rind is entirely up to you. Some older cheeses have tough rinds; however, they are edible. Bloomy rinds, such as the white coating on Brie and Camembert, are harmless; you don't have to dig under the skin to get the gooey goodness. Washed rinds, usually orange or red, may be pungent or salty, but they can be consumed. Wax rinds are the exception and best saved for your DIY candle project.

Why Does Your Cheese Look Like a Layer Cake?

Have you noticed that Morbier, the semisoft cow's-milk cheese named for a small town in France, has a horizontal line that resembles frosting in the middle of a layer cake?

The horizontal line is ash and its purpose is to separate the evening and morning milkings. In the old-time tradition, French cheese makers pressed the leftover evening curd into a mold and added a layer of ash on top of it to protect the cheese overnight. In the morning, additional curd was placed on top.

Many of the cheeses made these days use only one batch of milk, with the ash symbolically placed in the center.

If you're looking for a classically produced A.M./P.M. Morbier, ask your cheese-monger.

What Is Little Miss Muffet's Favorite Cheese?

We're all familiar with the nursery rhyme about little Miss Muffet sitting on her tuffet (a footstool, if you're wondering) and eating her curds and whey. But what exactly was in her bowl?

While it is impossible to know, a good guess is cottage cheese.

The dieter's staple is made of cheese curds, aka coagulated milk. The curds are heated in whey, then drained and rinsed. The last step is to add some liquid, usually milk or cream.

Cottage cheese is made from cow's milk and can range in fat content from 0 to 8 percent.

I don't mean to frighten you away, but if mold or an unpleasant odor occurs, you must throw away the cheese immediately. Otherwise, it should be good for seven to ten days in the refrigerator after it is opened.

Can You Cheddar All the Papers on Your Desk?

Cheddar cheese, the most popular cheese in America, was originally named for the village of the same name in Somerset County, England. However, the word *cheddar* is also known for the process, not a place.

The verb *cheddar,* a cheese-making term, means "to stack or layer."

When Cheddar is made, the curds are formed into slabs. The slabs are stacked upon one another, pressed, then turned and restacked. The entire process takes about ninety minutes.

Just as humans get sharper with age, so does Cheddar cheese. While it varies from producer to producer, a good guideline is that mild Cheddar has been ripened from two to four months, medium has aged four to eight months, sharp has aged nine to twelve months, and extra sharp has aged over one year.

Some Cheddar is so fresh that it squeaks when you bite into it. A Wisconsin invention, squeakers are bite-size Cheddar curds that are sold the day they are made. Just like day-old bread, squeakers must be labeled as such if they are more than twenty-four hours old.

For a final chuckle, let me tell you about truckle.

A truckle, which is either round or barrel-shaped, originated to use leftover milk after the big Cheddars were made. Today truckles have a less practical purpose and are considered an artisan cheese.

What Is Don Quixote's Favorite Cheese?

Manchego.

This buttery Spanish cheese hails from La Mancha, the land where Cervante's Don Quixote dwelled.

Manchego is one of Spain's most well known cheeses. It is made with whole milk from Manchego sheep exclusively in the La Mancha region. While there are "Manchego-style" cheeses made outside the region, it's easy to identify an authentic wheel by the basket-weave pattern around the sides. The label should be stamped "Manchego" or say that it was produced with 100 percent Manchego ewes' milk. To be certified it must age at least sixty days.

Manchego *curado* is aged for three to six months. If you're looking for something that has more time on the rind, choose the *viejo* ("old" in Spanish), which is aged nine to twelve months.

I wonder if Shakespeare was referring to Manchego when he wrote, "Can one desire too much of a good thing?"

Turo! Turo! Turo!

Although it sounds like the matadors' cry, *turo* has more to do with a dairy cow than a charging bull.

Turo is the Greek word for "cheese."

If you are a connoisseur of cheese, or even one that simply loves to eat cheese, then you qualify as a turophile.

The Science of Cheese

Quarks are among the tiniest particles in the universe. Even with an electron microscope, they are impossible to see. Murray Gell-Mann, the physicist who won the Nobel Prize in 1969 for discovering quarks and has a penchant for words, gave the particles their name from James Joyce's book *Finnegans Wake*.

Quark (pronounced "kwork") is not just a scientific term. It also has its place in cuisine—in German it means "curd," as in the substance to make cheese.

It's a quirky word with two distinct definitions, yet with all their differences, they have one commonality—flavors.

Quarks, the particles, have six "flavors": up, down, strange, charm, bottom, and top. Protons and neutrons are made from varying combinations of up quarks and down quarks.

Quark the cheese has one basic flavor: tangy. It's a cow's-milk cheese that tastes similar to sour cream.

Baked potato topped with quark or quark-bottom cheesecake, anyone?

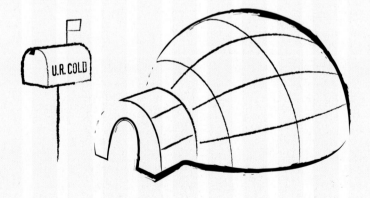

Aisle Four
frozen
food

IQF (It's Quite Fabulous) Skillet Cornbread ·75·

Lazy Latkes ·77·

What Can Buzz Lightyear Teach You About Your Freezer?

To infinity and beyond!

That's how long you can safely store frozen food. The USDA advises that food stored at a constant temperature of 0°F will be safe almost indefinitely. Safe, yes, but for taste and flavor, there *is* a shelf life.

The faster you get your food into the freezer, the better. The fresher the food is when frozen, the better it will taste when defrosted and prepared.

Ideally, keep your freezer at 0°F, cold enough to freeze a 2-inch item, such as a steak, in 2 hours. Never stack items to be frozen on top of each other. Wait until they are frozen solid.

Proper packaging is key. It's safe to freeze your meat or poultry in the butcher wrap, but only for a month or two. If you plan on freezing food for a longer time, wrap it a second time in heavy freezer foil or plastic wrap, then place it in a resealable bag, and date it.

Got freezer burn? It doesn't make food unsafe, just a little dry. Cut those white spots off and prepare as usual.

What about defrosting? The USDA Food Safety and Inspection Service provides these guidelines:

> Perishable foods should never be thawed on the counter or in hot water and must not be left at room temperature for more than 2 hours.
>
> Even though the center of the package may still be frozen as it thaws on the counter, the outer layer of the food could be in the "Danger Zone," between 40 and 140°F—temperatures at which bacteria multiply rapidly.
>
> When thawing frozen food, it's best to plan ahead and thaw in the refrigerator, where it will remain at a safe, constant temperature—at 40°F or below.
>
> There are three safe ways to thaw food: in the refrigerator, in cold water (must be in leak-proof packaging), and in the microwave.

For safety reasons, cook food defrosted in cold water or the micro immediately.

Epsicles

Nope, that's not a typo. The fruity frozen treat we know as a Popsicle was first called an Epsicle.

In 1905, Frank Epperson was eleven years old when he left a concoction of powdered soda mix and water in a cup outside on a winter night. When he awoke the next morning, it was frozen with the stirring stick upright in it.

When Frank had his own kids, he made Epsicles for them, but they called them Pop's Sicles. In 1923 Frank applied for a patent for his frozen drink on a stick and officially changed the name to Popsicle.

According to Popsicle.com (the official site for Popsicle), the twin pops that break apart were invented during the Depression, so kids could share one ice pop for five cents.

Why Should You Thank the Eskimos for Frozen Vegetables?

During a trip through the Arctic, adventurer Clarence Birdseye witnessed Eskimos freezing freshly caught fish using ice, wind, and cold temperatures. He realized the Eskimos' flash-freezing method preserved freshness, and he wanted to apply the same process to vegetables.

With the help of investors, Birdseye successfully replicated the Eskimos' process. By 1926 he had revolutionized the frozen-food industry with the introduction of his "Quick Freeze Machine." It froze vegetables so quickly that only small ice crystals would form, ensuring that the flavor, texture, and color of the vegetables were of the highest standard.

He didn't stop there. Birdseye also saw the need for a way to display his frozen vegetables. He developed the familiar freezer cases with the glass doors we see in grocery stores today.

I used to look down on frozen vegetables. That's until I learned most of them are frozen just hours after harvest, often making them "fresher" than those shipped from the farm to the market.

I-Scream!

An eight-year-old having a fit in 1920 is the reason we enjoy Eskimo Pies today.

The youngster had enough money for only one treat and couldn't decide between an ice cream sandwich and a chocolate candy bar. The dilemma got shop owner Christian Nelson thinking—why not combine the two?

Several weeks later Nelson had figured out how to keep the chocolate coating on the vanilla ice cream and called the new treat an I-Scream Bar. A clever pun and possibly a tribute to the boy who inspired it?

Nelson started looking for manufacturers and soon partnered with Russell Stover (of chocolate fame).

They received their patent in 1922 and renamed the novelty "Eskimo Pie." I don't know why the Eskimos received top billing when there were other Arctic names like "igloo," "penguin," and "polar bear" to choose from, although I'm pretty sure Avalanche Pie would not have been on their short list.

Ice-Cold Deep Fry

Adding cold items to hot oil reduces the oil's temperature and slows cooking. That's why recipes generally call for the food to be at room temperature before frying.

Ice water, however, is a critical ingredient if you are going to batter and fry, such as when you are making tempura. The cold water makes the tempura batter gummy, so that it works as an adhesive to keep the batter on the food item.

The basic tempura recipe is simple: 1 cup flour, 1 cup ice water, and 1 egg. Once you've made the batter, continue to keep it cold by putting the bowl with the batter on top of a larger bowl filled with ice.

The secret to the crunchy crust is that the flour hasn't absorbed much of the water before frying, so keep the mixing to a minimum to prevent the flour from sucking up too much liquid, and make it in batches just before you need it.

Tempura is tricky, so much so, that only senior chefs cook it in Japan.

Should You Bring Waffles to Church?

Before there was a waffle, there was a wafer, as in the Communion wafer or Christian Host offered at Eucharist.

It wasn't until the Middle Ages that secular bakeries were permitted to bake wafers, most likely to distinguish the laymen's leavened version from the unleavened Host. The secular leavened wafer became akin to the fluffy waffle we know today.

Fast-forward to the twentieth century and the brothers Dorsa from San Jose, California. In the early 1930s electric waffle irons were the newfangled gadget. The brothers created a prepared waffle batter, but when they ran into transportation issues with their fresh product, they switched to a dry mix that only required milk.

In the 1950s, when America started getting hungry for ready-to-eat frozen food, Frank Dorsa kept his waffle wonk going by inventing a contraption that could crank out masses of waffles a day. "Froffles" were frozen and shipped to supermarkets throughout the country.

How the breakfast treat later became known as "Eggos" hasn't been completely ironed out. Some say it's because the Dorsas' company name was Eggo, in honor of their first product, mayonnaise. Others claim it's because of the waffles' eggy flavor. Either way, "Leggo my Eggo" entered the American lexicon after Kellogg bought the company in 1970.

I wonder if a priest has ever said, "Leggo my wafer."

The IQ of IQF

The acronym IQF stands for "individually quick frozen." Food items are frozen individually then put together only after frozen solid. This technology is the reason that a bag of peas isn't one giant green block you have to hack apart with an ice pick.

IQF technology also locks in freshness. Seafood, such as shrimp, are sometimes IQFed on the boat, ensuring that they have their best flavor when defrosted.

You don't need a fancy IQF machine at home. I like to IQF the excess bounty from my summer garden. Whole tomatoes freeze beautifully when placed separately on a sheet pan. Once they are frozen, you can put them all together in a resealable plastic bag. They won't be slicing tomatoes anymore, but they are terrific for sauces.

Corn, one of the crown jewels of summer, is another one of my favorites to IQF. Remove the kernels with a sharp knife. I do this in a large wide bowl to keep them from spraying all over the counter.

Scatter the kernels on a sheet pan, taking special care that there are no clumps and none are touching each other. Once frozen, place them all in a resealable bag or freezer-safe container. You can use them for soups, chili, stews, and salads.

Berries are IQF candidates, too—either fresh from your garden or from the farmers' market. Freeze seasonal blueberries and strawberries the day you harvest or buy them. (Be sure you rinse them in cool water and pat dry first. Hull strawberries.)

You'll smile in winter when you are enjoying the bounty from the summer.

IQF (It's Quite Fabulous) Skillet Cornbread

Serves 10 to 12

If I had to pick just one pan to cook with for the rest of my life, it would be versatile cast iron. When my dear pal Lucy Young passed away, her husband, Bill, offered me anything I wanted as remembrance, including jewelry, but I chose her sixty-year-old seasoned cast-iron skillet instead. Bill had it engraved for me and it remains a treasured part of my kitchen.

1 cup flour, plus ¼ cup for dusting corn kernels

1 cup cornmeal

1 teaspoon baking powder

1 teaspoon baking soda

1 teaspoon salt

2 large eggs

1½ cups buttermilk

4 tablespoons melted butter

½ cup honey

2 cups IQF corn kernels (yours or from the frozen section)

2 tablespoons butter

✤ Preheat the oven to 450°F.

✤ Place 1 cup flour and the cornmeal, baking powder, baking soda, and salt in a large bowl. Stir to combine.

✤ In a separate bowl, lightly beat the eggs. Whisk in the buttermilk (shake well before measuring), melted butter, and honey.

✤ Pour the wet ingredients into the dry ingredients. Stir gently with a rubber spatula.

✤ Place ¼ cup flour on a plate and lightly dust the frozen corn kernels. Put the corn in a colander or sieve and shake off all the excess flour. Mix the corn into the batter, stirring until just combined.

✤ Heat a cast-iron skillet to medium-high heat and melt the 2 tablespoons butter.

✤ As soon as the butter is melted and bubbling (don't let it burn), turn off the heat. Immediately pour the batter into the hot skillet. Place the skillet on the middle rack of the oven.

✤ Bake until golden brown and a toothpick inserted in the center comes out clean, about 20 minutes. (It's okay if it's a tad jiggly in the center.)

✤ Remove the skillet from the oven and cool on a wire rack until completely set, 15 to 20 minutes.

✤ Cut the cornbread into wedges and serve with softened butter and honey.

FROZEN FOOD

Can't Make Ends Meet?

Neither could the owners of Ore-Ida.

In 1953, Ore-Ida's founders, the Grigg brothers, were looking for a way to repurpose the slivers of potatoes that were left over after making French fries. Ever the innovators, they shredded the pieces, added onion and seasonings, molded them into a drumlike shape, fried them, and dubbed them Tater Tots®.

Ore-Ida gets its name from the two neighboring states where the potatoes for its products are grown: Oregon and Idaho.

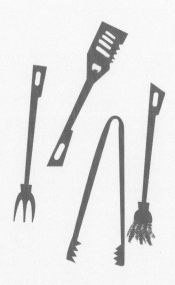

Lazy Latkes

8 latkes

Most of my pals when I was growing up were either Jewish or Greek, and I loved to eat dinner at their houses. Mrs. Hirsch was the first person to serve me a latke. I was taken aback by the savory potato pancake (it wasn't what I expected), but soon the crispy crust and snap of the onion won me over. Making latkes from scratch is labor intensive. However, one night, to celebrate Hanukkah with one of my daughter's friends, I created a shortcut using Tater Tots®.

2 cups Tater Tots® potatoes

¼ cup onions, minced

½ cup matzo meal

1 teaspoon salt

Ground pepper to taste

3 eggs, lightly beaten

Vegetable oil for browning

Sour cream

Applesauce

✦ Defrost the Tater Tots® potatoes by spreading them in one layer on sheet pan. When they are defrosted, break them up into a large bowl. Mix in the onions, matzo meal, salt, and pepper. Add the beaten eggs and mix thoroughly with a fork.

✦ Form the mixture into patties ½ inch thick. Use enough oil to generously cover the bottom of a skillet and cook the patties over medium heat until golden brown on both sides.

✦ Drain the latkes on paper towels and plate. Serve with sides of sour cream and applesauce.

TATER TOTS is a registered trademark owned by H.J. Heinz Company and is used with permission.

FROZEN FOOD

Aisle Five
fish and seafood

Why Should You Put Shrimp in Your First-Aid Box?

Shrimp shells contain chitosan, a compound that can help clot wounds.

Knowing this, HemCon Medical Technologies developed a special bandage to help stop hemorrhaging on the battlefield.

The bandage contains a scientific mixture of chitosan, extracted from shrimp shells, that stops severe bleeding in as little as two minutes. Another advantage is that the unique bandages adhere to wet wounds and are naturally antibacterial.

HemCon bandages have been used by the U.S. armed forces and in hospitals for years. One day they may reach consumers. Be on the lookout for Shrimp-Aids, er, HemCon bandages, in pharmacies and stores soon.

You Won't Get Plump with These Prawns

Serves 8 to 10

Prawns are low in calories and high in protein, perfect for my healthy lifestyle. I use endive in many recipes to replace toast points or crackers. Save the calories and the carbs where you can!

1 cup raw shrimp, about ½ pound, peeled and deveined

1 lemon

2 tablespoons shallot, minced

1 tablespoon fresh dill, minced

1 teaspoon olive oil

Salt

Freshly ground black pepper

3 heads endive

✤ Cut the ends off the lemon, remove the zest, and juice the lemon, reserving the zest and juice.

✤ Place the shrimp in a saucepan, cover with water, and add the lemon end pieces. Cook uncovered. As soon as the shrimp turn pink, remove them from the heat, drain, and place them in a bath of ice water.

✤ Remove the shrimp from the ice-water bath. Pat the shrimp dry, chop them, and put them in a bowl. Add the minced shallot, dill, and lemon zest. Pour just enough olive oil over the mixture to coat it. Season to taste with lemon juice, salt, and pepper.

✤ Separate and trim the endive leaves. Place 1 teaspoon of shrimp in the bed of each endive leaf. Chill until ready to serve.

What Can STP Tell You About Your Scallops?

Mario Andretti won the 1969 Indy 500 in an STP-sponsored racecar. In case you don't know, STP is a motor-oil treatment.

When it comes to treatment of your scallops, you'll want to know about another STP: sodium tripolyphosphate.

There are wet and dry (I don't mean dried) scallops. The scallops that are white and stand straight up are treated with STP to retain added water and to preserve them. They are known as wet scallops, because of the saltwater solution they are soaked in. There are three characteristics of STP-treated scallops: they are slick and slippery, they are shiny in appearance, and if they are purchased in a container, the liquid might foam.

The ones that may look less appealing, dull really, slightly tacky, droopy, and have little or no liquid, are dry scallops and are more desirable.

How Do You Know When You Need More Mussel?

What do you do when you get home and notice that some of the mussels you purchased are open? Do you return them? Replace them? Throw them out? How do you know if the mussels are safe to eat?

According to Chef Corky Clark, Culinary Institute of America professor, they are okay if they are open, as long as you can at least partially reclose the shell. The shell will only yield if the mussel is still alive. Discard any that remain open, because they're not sleepy—they're dead. Mussels should be alive until just before cooking. Since removing the beard kills them, that should be the last step before putting them in the pot.

What about mussels that do not open after they are cooked? It probably means that they are "mudders"—literally full of mud—and you'll have to give them the heave-ho.

Be Cool at the Fish Counter

In 2002, the USDA was charged by Congress with the establishment of mandatory rules for the labeling of fish and shellfish.

The result was COOL—it stands for Country of Origin Labeling—and it went into effect in April 2005. Knowing where your wild fish comes from is important, but the Country of Origin mandate is a bit tricky. It means the country where the boat is from, not the waters where the fish was caught.

When it comes to farm-raised fish, the rules are more stringent. If it is identified as coming from the United States, it must be raised, harvested, and processed in American waters.

It's cool to be smart. The next time you are choosing seafood, look for the tags stuck in the ice next to the fish, the ones that have the price on them. They should indicate the name of the fish, where the fish came from, and if the fish is farmed or wild, another of the COOL mandates. If you don't see that information clearly labeled or if the fishmonger is crabby and not complying, it might be time to find another market.

What Does a Dead Man Know About Tuna?

I used to think that eating sashimi on a boat, just sliced from a freshly caught tuna, was the pinnacle of freshness and flavor. Freshness yes, but flavor, not so much.

My pal Gary Chu, chef and owner of Osake restaurant, taught me that two-day-old tuna tastes better than tuna caught the same day.

That's because once the tuna is caught and killed, it goes into a state of rigor mortis, meaning that all the muscles stiffen. The flavor improves a few days later when the muscles relax again.

Why Did the Lobster Cross the Road?

All riddles aside, there are poultry references for lobsters.

A female lobster is known as a hen and a lobster weighing less than 1 pound is called a chicken.

So why did the lobster cross the road?

Because her roe boat was broken.

Lox Versus Smoked Salmon

Both lox and smoked salmon are smoked, but at different temperatures and for different lengths of time. In cold smoking, the temperature ranges from 70 to 90°F. In hot smoking, temperatures vary from 120 to 180°F. Hot smoking is a faster process than cold smoking. Hot smoked fish will not last as long as cold smoked fish.

Lightly smoked fish, regardless of the temperature in which it was prepared, is good in the fridge for a few days or a few weeks.

Lox is cured in brine and cold-smoked.

Nova or Nova Scotia salmon is just another name for cold-smoked salmon.

Male Versus Female Lobster

Tom's favorite dinner is a whole steamed lobster. He prefers the flavor of female lobster and the roe that occasionally comes with it. Apparently it's not an unusual request, because although I giggle every time he orders a female, the waiters never flinch.

How do you make certain you were served the lobster you ordered? By identifying the swimmerets, those flippers on the bottom of the lobster near the tail.

On females the swimmerets are feathery and delicate. Their tails tend to be broader. Male lobsters have hard and boney swimmerets, and their tails are narrow.

The Pocket Fisherman

A rod and reel that fit in your back pocket was all the rage in the 1970s and 1980s. Now there is a new pocket fisherman for the twenty-first century.

Thanks to the Monterey Bay Aquarium Seafood Watch, you can download and print a pocket guide, or download an application on your smart phone, that will help you make ocean-friendly seafood choices.

Each *Seafood Watch* pocket guide is created for a specific region. You can find a guide for where you live or where you are traveling. There is also a sushi guide.

The United States imports about 80 percent of our seafood. Making environmentally friendly decisions when purchasing fish helps support abundant and healthy oceans.

What Do Your Dyed-to-Match Shoes Have in Common with Farm-Raised Salmon?

All farm-raised salmon contain added color.

Since farmed salmon do not eat a diet of colorful krill like wild salmon, their flesh is gray. Salmon farmers add dye to the fish food, which turns the color of their flesh into the "natural" pigment of wild salmon. Fish farmers use a color chart with over thirty selections to determine the hue of their salmon, so some are pink and others are orange. It's similar to choosing colors of shoes to match bridesmaid dresses.

The FDA requires that retailers disclose that color has been added. If you see "farm raised" on the salmon tag, and it doesn't list "added color," then something fishy is going on.

Simple Salmon Met the Parchment

Serves 4

I've used foil packets on the grill for years, but ever since parchment paper came to my pantry, I've prepared dinner with less muss and fuss right in the oven.

2 cups cherry tomatoes, halved (ideally a mixture of red and yellow cherry and pear tomatoes, or Nature Sweet Cherubs)

2 green onions, thinly sliced

2 tablespoons olive oil

½ teaspoon Spanish paprika

½ teaspoon salt

Pepper to taste

4 (4-ounce) wild salmon fillets, center cut

✤ Preheat the oven to 450°F.

✤ Combine the tomatoes, green onions, olive oil, paprika, salt, and pepper. Let the mixture stand on counter 10 to 15 minutes. Do not refrigerate.

✤ Tear four 12-inch-wide pieces of parchment paper. Place each salmon fillet in the center of a parchment piece. Put one-fourth of the tomato mixture on top and around the sides of the fish. Bring the sides of the parchment up to form a tent shape. Fold the edges of the parchment over ½ inch and keep folding the parchment down until it is about 2 inches over the salmon. Twist the ends. Repeat for the other three pieces.

✤ Place all four packets on a cookie sheet or sheet pan. Bake for 12 minutes for medium rare (my preference) or longer until desired doneness.

✤ Carefully open the packets to let the steam escape. Remove the salmon from the parchment and place on warm plates. Place tomatoes on top. Serve immediately.

Fish X-Rays

Fish processors "candle" their fish to check for worms, especially skinless fish whose flesh is thin, such as cod. The candling box looks like the light box doctors use to read X-rays, except it is on a table, not the wall. When the fish fillet is illuminated, it is easy to detect worms, and they are removed before the fish comes to market.

Ever since I first saw this demonstrated at the Culinary Institute of America, I always double check that my cod has been candled by holding it up to the brightest light in my kitchen. If I find any worms, and I have, I remove them, reminding myself all along that cooking will kill anything I missed.

How Do You Turn a Day-Old Fish into a Four-Day-Old Fish in an Instant?

For every 2 degrees above 32°F that you store your fish for one day, it loses one day of shelf life.

Most home refrigerators hover around 40°F. So if you bought tilapia on Monday, flopped it in the fridge, and didn't eat it until Tuesday's dinner, the fish instantly aged four days. However, if you store your fish between the freezing point of water, 32°F, and the freezing point of fish, 28°F, your fish will remain true to its age.

When you get home, wrap your fish in parchment if possible. If you don't have any, that's fine. Either way, put the fish in a plastic bag, but please *never* seal it. Sealing traps gasses and encourages the fishy odor. Set the bag on a plate of ice (be sure it's folded so that melted ice can't get in), then place a light amount of ice on top of the fish. Store it in the coldest part of your refrigerator.

It goes without saying that if you purchased your seafood at the market, you probably don't know how old it is, so it's best eaten that day. Be sure to ice it immediately to preserve flavor and freshness until it's time to prepare it.

Heads You Win, Tails You Lose

Removing pin bones from fish can be tricky. The secret is to always pull the bones out toward the head using tweezers or needle-nose pliers. If you pull toward the tail, the bones will snap and the delicate flesh will rip.

If you have a whole fish, the head will be obvious, but what to do with a fillet? If it's a round fish fillet, such as salmon or Spanish mackerel, lay the fillet, skin side down, over the back of a small bowl. The pin bones will show you the way.

"Filet" is the English spelling, and "fillet" is the French spelling. It's acceptable to pronounce fillet "fill-it" or "fill-ay." Filet, with one *l*, is pronounced "fill-ay."

Do Lobsters Carry Concealed Weapons?

Lobsters that have no claws are called pistols. Their meat is delicious despite the deformity. Culls are lobsters with one claw.

If you're not presenting your lobster whole on a platter, you'll get more bang for your buck by using pistols and culls. Their chopped meat works well in many recipes, such as lobster rolls and salads.

Scraping by with Sushi

You probably wouldn't call eating sushi scraping by—it's expensive and something of a luxury. That said, scraping might affect your spicy tuna rolls.

Tuna scrape is manufactured in India. The process utilizes the fish left on the tuna's skeleton after all the big and expensive pieces have been cut off. Waste not, want not, right?

Although it sounds thrifty to use every scrap of fish, tuna scrape can be more dangerous than thrifty. The pickings from the tuna bones are combined with remnants from other fish and frozen in blocks. While it is supposed to be safe, the chopped mixture is not treated with anything to destroy bacteria. It is shipped from India to the United States, and despite FDA regulations for imported food, only a fraction of the fish is actually inspected.

Add to this not-so-pretty picture that we consume this product raw, and you can see that it might not be worth the risk.

How do you know if you are eating scrape, when it's in a roll mixed with spices and avocado?

You won't be getting it at reputable sushi bars, which offer a high-quality grade of tuna that is sliced in front of you. It's called Nakaochi scrape, although it may not be labeled that way. Be on the lookout for it in sushi rolls at convenience stores and supermarkets.

Can Your Frying Pan Help You Choose Safe Fish?

If the whole fish (or the size it was before it was cut into fillets) fits in a 10- or 12-inch frying pan, it's probably low in mercury.

That's because the amount of mercury increases in a fish the more it eats, the longer it lives, and the bigger it gets.

General guidelines say that smaller and younger fish contain the lowest amount of mercury. Those include catfish, cod, rainbow trout, wild salmon, tilapia, lobster, oysters, and shrimp. Fish high in mercury are swordfish, shark, king mackerel, and tilefish.

It is important to note that cooking, even at high heat, does not reduce or eliminate mercury.

But don't scale back on your consumption of seafood. The National Academy of Sciences states in the study *Toxicological Effects of Methylmercury* (2000):

> *Because of the beneficial effects of fish consumption, the long-term goal needs to be a reduction in the concentrations of mercury in fish rather than the replacement of fish in the diet by other foods. In the interim, the best method of maintaining fish consumption and minimizing mercury exposure is the consumption of fish known to have lower methylmercury concentrations.*

Now you are in-tuna with healthy fish purchasing practices.

Shrimp Phlebotomist?

When you have your blood drawn, it is sometimes difficult to find the vein. The same is true with shrimp.

The black vein that runs down the back of the curved shell is the shrimp's intestinal tract. How prominent it is may depend on whether the shrimp was farm-raised or wild.

Farm-raised shrimp have a small vein. That's because they don't eat much in captivity and are not fed before harvest. Wild shrimp, on the other hand, are hearty eaters and will have a thick, sandy vein.

Either way, remove the vein in all but the smallest shrimp.

Speaking of size, what do numbers like 16/20 mean? Shrimp are measured by a count (number). The numbers reflect approximately how many shrimp of that size will create a pound. Making the math easy: 16/20 means 16 to 20 shrimps are in that pound. The shrimpy shrimp have the biggest numbers and the jumbos have the smallest.

What Do Captain Sig Hansen of _Deadliest Catch_ and a Manhole Cover Have in Common?

King crab.

Captain Sig is a fourth-generation king crab fisherman. He spends October to January in the Bering Sea, catching king crab on his boat, _The Northwestern_.

King crab has a wingspan, er, leg span of as much as 5 feet. Only male king crab is allowed to be harvested. That may explain why a typical king crab is as big as a manhole cover.

Despite the count of eight appendages, only six are legs. The other two are claws, and they are not as prized for their meat.

King crab is measured by how many legs it takes to make 10 pounds. That number averages from 12 to 14, but imagine if it were 1 to 2. Those would be giant legs! And when it comes to king crab, bigger is better.

King crab sold in the United States is already cooked. When preparing it, be careful not to reheat it too harshly or its delicate flavor will be ruined.

FISH AND SEAFOOD

Captain Sig's Crab Rangoon

About 30 pieces

When Captain Sig was a guest on *The Food Guy and Marcy Show,* I was surprised to learn that eating king crab was a treat for him. Between the effort to catch it and the high price it fetches, he doesn't eat it very often. This is my take on crab Rangoon, a classic that can stretch a small amount of crab a long way. It pairs well with sparkling wine and mai tais. Or with Captain Sig's favorite cocktail, Norwegian Champagne—a mixture of Coca Cola and vodka.

---

1 cup crabmeat

4 ounces cream cheese, at room temperature

1 green onion, finely minced

2 to 4 pearl-size drops of Sriracha hot chili sauce

1 (12-ounce) package square wonton skins

Vegetable oil for frying

Chinese mustard

Sweet and sour sauce

✤ Blend the crab with the cream cheese. Add the green onion and Sriracha.

✤ To wrap the wontons, dip your finger in a bowl of water and outline the edges of the wonton skin. Place a teaspoon of crab mixture in the center. Don't overfill. Fold the skin in half to make a triangle, sealing the edges well. Continue working with it in this position, with the point at the top. Bring the side corners over to the center and press down firmly.

✤ Fill a pan 1 inch deep with oil and heat over medium-high heat. Dip the edge of a wonton skin in the oil. If it sizzles, the oil is ready. Fry six to eight pieces at time until slightly golden brown. Drain on paper towels.

✤ Serve with Chinese mustard and sweet and sour sauce.

My Lovely Bones

My pal Chef Constantinos "Taki" Laliotitis is to blame, or should receive credit, for my carcass-saving heroics.

During a break recording *The Food Guy and Marcy Show* at the Kendall-Jackson Wine Center, I wandered into the kitchen and saw him prepping bouillabaisse. Next to his seafood were neat piles of shrimp shells, empty crab knuckles, and lobster exoskeletons. He explained that when he doesn't have the time to make stock right away (like most of us), he always freezes shells and bones. To do anything else would be wasteful and, in my words, not his, a culinary sin.

Ever since then, no matter how tired or lazy I am, I cannot bring myself to throw away bones or shells, and that's saying a lot from someone who uses rotisserie chicken and shrimp on a regular basis.

My freezer may look like a graveyard, but at least I always have the skeletal ingredients for a variety of stocks.

Why It's Important to Clam Up

There is a reason that "clam" is both a noun and a verb. The verb derives from "clamp" and means "to shut," and that's very important when choosing clams.

Hard-neck clams, such as Littleneck or Cherrystone, should have tightly closed shells when you purchase them. If the clam is slightly open, tap it; if the shell snaps shut, it is safe to eat. Any clams that remain open even a smidge have gone to the great clambake in the sky and need to be discarded.

Never store clams in freshwater or in an airtight environment. A well-ventilated container (such as a colander) covered with a wet paper towel is recommended.

Littlenecks and Longnecks

The best clams I've ever eaten were on the beach in Cabo San Lucas, freshly caught and steamed, and enjoyed with an ice-cold beer. These little beauties taste like a big bowl of Baja.

Serves 6

½ pound uncooked chorizo

2 tablespoons butter

2 tablespoons olive oil

1 shallot, minced

4 cloves of garlic, thinly sliced

1 (12-ounce) bottle of longneck beer, your choice

2 pounds hard-neck clams, washed (see "Flour Power," page 122) then scrubbed under cold running water to remove all sand

¼ cup cilantro, minced

✤ Heat a heavy skillet (one that has a lid) over medium heat. Remove the chorizo from the casing and break it into chunks. Crumble it as it cooks, about 10 minutes. Remove the chorizo from the pan to a plate lined with paper towels to drain excess oil. Do not clean the skillet.

✤ Return the skillet to the stove. Melt the butter and olive oil over medium-low heat. Add the shallots and garlic. Cook until soft and aromatic, scraping up the bits of chorizo that are left in the skillet at the same time, about 3 minutes. Add the chorizo and mix well. Pour in the bottle of beer and bring the liquid to a boil.

✤ Reduce the heat to medium-low. Add the clams. Cover and cook until the clams are open, about 5 to 7 minutes. Discard any clams that are closed.

✤ Serve in bowls with plenty of broth, garnished with cilantro.

✤ I call liquid that is left over after cooking NOG—Nectar of the Gods. This clam NOG screams for warm crusty bread, garlic bread, or fried polenta.

Aisle Six
dressings, marinades, condiments, spices

Want to Tenderize Your Meat? Take It to the ER!

Marinating does not tenderize food. Trauma does!

Jim Tarantino advises in his book *Marinades* that the acidic content of citrus, wine, or vinegar only softens meat: "The word 'tender' carries the connotation of being warm, caring, and sensitive; tenderizing is anything but. It's about controlled food damage, and it can happen in food when muscle tissue is separated, torn, or bruised."

To get meat truly tender, use a flat mallet or meat-tenderizing hammer.

Marinades are flavor boosters, but at their best they only penetrate the surface of the food up to ¼ inch. Many factors determine how quickly your marinade will work. The colder the temperature, the longer it takes. The denser the meat, the longer you'll have to wait.

In a hurry? The more you cover your meat in marinade, the faster the process.

Russian Versus Thousand Island

What's the difference between Russian dressing and Thousand Island?

Russian is the original, and Thousand Island is the variation. Both start with basic mixtures of mayonnaise and ketchup or chili sauce. However, Thousand Island includes finely chopped pickles or relish.

Russian dressing isn't Russian. It's American in origin. *The Food Lover's Companion* suggests that it may have been called Russian dressing because early recipes contained caviar, Russia's famous export.

But how did Thousand Island get its name? Legend has it that Thousand Island was named for the specks of relish, which look like tiny islands. Another theory suggests the dressing was created and named in the New York fishing community known as the Thousand Islands.

Can Ketchup Get a Speeding Ticket?

The Heinz® website reports that ketchup coming out of the glass bottle any faster than .028 miles per hour is rejected for sale. That's too fast to meet the company's standards. Although they may not issue a citation, they do require a certain thickness and viscosity to be certified as Heinz® Tomato Ketchup.

Ever been stuck trying to get the thick ketchup out of a glass bottle? Here's a secret that works every time. Firmly tap the "57" on the neck of the bottle.

The ketchup will flow freely, and you may become a hero to a frustrated fry eater.

While we're on the subject, why the 57? Founder Henry Heinz chose it somewhat arbitrarily. Although he made over 60 products by 1896, he liked the number 57 and thought it was lucky.

More than a hundred years later, Heinz® manufactures more than 5,700 products worldwide, but so far they haven't added two zeros after the original 57 on the iconic ketchup bottle.

Mupcakes

12 Mupcakes

I started making these mini meatloaves baked in a muffin pan when my kids were little. I added the V8 juice for the extra nutrients and soon discovered it was a terrific flavor booster. These are convenient for potlucks, because they provide individual servings.

1 pound 90/10 ground sirloin

½ pound ground pork

½ cup unseasoned breadcrumbs

1 teaspoon garlic powder

¾ teaspoon salt

1 egg, slightly beaten

¼ cup V8 Original Vegetable Juice

½ cup minced onion

1 tablespoon butter

½ cup HEINZ® Tomato Ketchup

1 tablespoon packed brown sugar

½ to 1 teaspoon Worcestershire sauce

✤ Preheat the oven to 350°F.

✤ In a large mixing bowl, place the ground beef, ground pork, bread-crumbs, garlic powder, salt, egg, and V8 juice. Sauté onions in butter until softened, about 5 minutes. Add them to the mixture. Working with your hands, combine all the ingredients, but do not overmix. Fill each muffin cup ¾ full.

✤ Bake for 10 minutes. In the meantime, combine the remaining three ingredients. Brush the glaze generously on the Mupcakes and continue baking for 15 minutes more.

✤ Lift the Mupcakes out of muffin pan with tongs and place on paper towels to drain any excess oil. Allow to rest for 10 minutes.

HEINZ is a registered trademark owned by H.J. Heinz Company and is used with permission.

Why Should You Bring Mustard to the Gym?

Mustard is tasty on hot dogs, and it's a weight-loss tool too.

Dr. Jaya Henry, of England's Oxford Polytechnic Institute, says that 1 teaspoon of mustard can speed up the metabolic rate by 20 to 25 percent. That's equivalent to your body burning approximately 45 more calories for every 700 calories consumed.

Spicy mustards are the key here—the type you typically find in Asian markets or are called for in Mexican or Indian recipes. Don't stop those bench presses—the metabolic effect is temporary and similar to the boost you get from caffeine in coffee.

For fitness funsters like myself, I'll take any advantage I can get, including mustard.

Bailing Out the Mayo

I have potluck phobia. It only took one run-in with food poisoning to have me cease and desist. It was potato salad at a picnic. There was no trial—I declared the mayonnaise to be the culprit.

It turns out that I was too quick to judge; it wasn't the mayo after all. Commercially prepared mayonnaise contains vinegar and lemon juice. The acidity, combined with salt, actually retards food spoilage and prevents bacterial growth.

Blame the meat, poultry, fish, or eggs. If any of those had been kept out of the refrigerator more than 2 hours, it would have been the most likely offender.

Spice Up Your Travel

It's no secret that airline food never tastes great, but you may not know that it is partly because your taste buds dull at 35,000 feet.

With the cabin pressure and low humidity, our sense of smell is compromised and therefore our ability to taste is affected. It's like eating with a bad cold. Appreciation of sweet and salty foods is lessened by up to 30 percent; sour foods tend to taste the same whether on the ground or in the air.

We have Lufthansa to thank for the research. It owns one of the world's largest simulators in which to measure how cabin conditions effect our perceptions of taste.

Another interesting study was conducted by Unilever R&D in collaboration with the University of Manchester. The report said:

> *It seems people lose their sense of taste when listening to white noise. When the participants liked the background sound, it enhanced their enjoyment of the flavor of the food. When they disliked the background sound, it reduced their enjoyment. This may help to explain the poor reputation of airline food, where the drone of the engines may interfere with the pleasure of eating.*

Based on these conclusions, your food may taste better on an airplane if you wear noise-reducing headphones.

Airline chefs do their best to create tasty meals, but you may want to do what I do—bring packets of hot sauce with you to spice up the bland fare or, if necessary, camouflage the taste. Since the TSA bans bringing liquids weighing more than 3 ounces on board, I collect the packets at to-go counters and save them for my plane trips.

Dark Soy Sauce Versus Light Soy Sauce

It's more than just the color.

Dark soy sauce is aged longer than light soy. Sometimes molasses is added to it, resulting in a sweeter flavor than regular soy sauce. It's often used in long-cooking or braised dishes.

Light soy sauce is thinner, saltier, and paler in color than the dark. It is typically used in stir-fries and marinades and as a dipping sauce.

Umami Chicken Salad

Serves 4

When I was a film student at UCLA, I interned with director Charles Dubin on the final season of *M*A*S*H*. My favorite lunch at the 20th Century Fox commissary was the Chinese Chicken Salad. The dressing was not typical—it was thick and creamy, not sweet and thin. It was umami before there was umami.

DRESSING

1 cup mayonnaise

2 tablespoons soy sauce

1 teaspoon Worcestershire

Juice of 1 lemon

2 teaspoons ground ginger

SALAD

3 cups Napa cabbage, shredded

3 cups romaine hearts, thinly sliced

2 cups rotisserie chicken, shredded

1 large celery stalk, sliced on the diagonal

2 green onions, thinly sliced

½ red bell pepper, diced

DRESSING

✢ Mix all the ingredients together well.

SALAD

✢ Place the salad ingredients in a large bowl. Pour the dressing on the salad and toss with salad tongs.

✢ If you're still craving more crunch, top with sliced almonds, chopped cashews, or fried chow mein noodles.

Eat to Your Heart's Desire

If you have elevated triglycerides, Penn State's researcher Sheila West has good news for you. Curry, garlic, turmeric, rosemary, oregano, paprika, and black pepper are all spices that can significantly reduce triglyceride levels.

To prove it, Ms. West recruited several nonsqueamish diners willing to eat the spicy test food and have their blood drawn several times, too. The subjects, all overweight men, were fed a fairly high-fat meal on the first night. The next day, they were served the same meal; however, it was prepared with 2 tablespoons of spices. The before and after blood tests were analyzed, and the results were startling. Triglycerides were lowered by as much as 30 percent after the spicy meal.

Spices associated with dessert, like cinnamon and cloves, also have the beneficial effect.

I am not a doctor, nor do I play one in this book, but as the data emerges, you may be able to reduce your risk of heart disease while eating your favorite high-fat foods—as long as they are prepared with a generous amount of spices.

Paprika onion rings, anyone?

What Cue Should Your Salt Take from the Tea Party?

When you think of salt, think of the Tea Party. Conservative.

You know how hard it is to take back something you said? It's even harder with salt.

Top Chef taught me, "Taste as you cook." I can't tell you how many times I added salt at the beginning, only to realize it was too much and it was too late to correct it. Add salt only as you need it.

Maybe it's too much food television, but now I have my salt bowls (sea salt, kosher, Maldon) by the stove. That way I can sprinkle it with my fingers from a foot or two above the food instead of using a shaker. That gives me a much better sense of how much I am using. Plus it gives me the illusion of being a cheftestant.

How do you rescue a dish when you've oversalted it? There's a lot of debate about that. Acids, like lemon juice or vinegar, are sometimes used. Peeled potatoes are rumored to absorb excess salt, but that won't cut it with Padma.

If you don't want to hear, "Please pack your knives and go," salt as you go, and taste, taste, taste.

The Skinny on Dressing

If you want to lose weight, do you order the salad dressing on the side? Do you believe that if you portion it yourself, you'll save calories?

I hate to rock your romaine, but my experience proves otherwise. I went from fatty to fit several years ago, and now I always ask the kitchen to toss my salad.

I had my epiphany when my chef pals told me they put more dressing in the ramekin that accompanies the salad than they use tossing it in the kitchen. If you order your dressing on the side, keep that in mind before finishing it all.

Unless you are one of those dip-the-fork-in-the-dressing-and-dab-it-on-your-lettuce types, do what I do and request your salad "lightly tossed." Your leaves will be evenly and delicately coated, an effect hard to achieve at the table using flatware and a small serving bowl. It's all about using less dressing and saving calories, so send the salad back if it is soaked.

Should You Dab Tabasco Sauce Behind Your Ears and on Your Wrists?

Edmund McIlhenny, living on Avery Island in Louisiana in the 1860s, was bored with the humdrum diet of the day. Looking to improve the flavor of his daily meals, he created a sauce using peppers from his garden, French white wine vinegar, and Avery Island salt.

According to family lore, McIlhenny packaged his pepper sauce in discarded cologne bottles fitted with a sprinkler on the lid, so it could be sprinkled rather than poured. It was so popular with his friends and family that they dubbed it, "The Famous Sauce Mr. McIlhenny Makes." This gave him the impetus to manufacture it commercially. Initially he wanted to call it Petite Anse Sauce, after the family island, but when his family resisted, he settled on his second choice, Tabasco, a word of Mexican Indian origin meaning "land where the soil is humid" (just like Avery Island's climate) or "place of the coral or oyster shell."

In 1868, McIlhenny produced 658 bottles of Tabasco in new "cologne bottles," a term of affection that he continued to use as his business grew. More than one hundred and forty years later, the Tabasco sauce recipe remains largely the same, and it's still made on Avery Island, where it's barrel aged for up to three years.

Tabasco sauce does not need to be refrigerated (but should be stored in a cool place away from direct light) and has a shelf life of up to five years. In case you don't have the time or wherewithal to count, there are at least 720 drops of Tabasco sauce in every 2-ounce bottle.

Grandma Mary's Secret Prime Rib Sauce

A generous amount for a crowd

I have been cutting recipes from newspapers for twenty-five years. I have a huge stack of clippings. However, there are a few I pull out every year, including this one. Pacific Market in Santa Rosa published this on December 20, 2000, in *The Press Democrat*. Simply put, it's a stunner. I serve it every Christmas with prime rib. Grandma Mary's grandson and Pacific Market owner Ken Silveira allowed me to share this recipe as a tribute to his grandmother.

1 pound sliced mushrooms

20 chopped green onions

¼ cup Worcestershire sauce

½ cup Kitchen Bouquet

16 drops Tabasco sauce

1⅓ cups ketchup

1 cup white wine

1 cup sherry

4 teaspoons chili powder

8 tablespoons sugar

6 teaspoons salt

4 teaspoons pepper

6 ounces (1½ sticks) butter

✤ Combine all ingredients and simmer 2 hours.

A lot of vintage recipes, especially those handed down from generations, didn't include instructions. These are the steps I use:

✤ Melt the butter.

✤ Sauté the mushrooms and green onions over medium-low heat for 5 to 7 minutes.

✤ Add the remaining ingredients and simmer for 2 hours.

What Salad Dressing Will You Find in the Theater?

William Archer wrote the play *Green Goddess*. The Broadway hit (later a film) starred George Arliss and had a run in San Francisco. While George was performing there, he dined regularly at the Palace Hotel. In 1923 executive chef Phillip Roemer created Green Goddess Dressing in honor of him.

The original recipe blended mayonnaise, sour cream, chives, parsley, lemon juice, vinegar, white wine, anchovies, salt, and ground pepper.

Nearly a century later, Green Goddess is having an encore. American restaurants are reviving the dressing and putting it back on their menus.

John's Green Goddess Dressing

1½ cups

My pal John Lasseter, the one who insisted I write this book, loves Green Goddess dressing. He first had it in Southern California at Bob's Big Boy restaurant. (John and I still make pilgrimages to Bob's Big Boy in Burbank; during the weekdays you may spot a celebrity or two, as many of the major studios are nearby.) For a limited time in the 1980s the dressing was available in supermarkets. Unfortunately it was phased out after a few years, and he's been craving it ever since. The green theme goes deeper—it's John's favorite color. That's why Buzz Lightyear (from John's first movie, *Toy Story*) has green on his space ranger uniform. I re-created this green classic in John's honor.

1 clove garlic

½ cup mayonnaise

½ cup sour cream

½ avocado, chopped

¼ cup English cucumber, peel on, chopped

2 tablespoons fresh tarragon, chopped

1 tablespoon chives, chopped

1 bunch watercress, chopped

1 tablespoon lemon juice

¼ teaspoon sea salt or celery salt, or to taste

Salt and pepper, to taste

✤ Using a food processor or blender, pulse the garlic until finely minced. Add the mayo, sour cream, avocado, and cucumber. Blend until completely smooth. Add the tarragon, chives, watercress, and lemon juice. Blend until creamy.

✤ Transfer to a bowl. Mix in sea salt or celery salt. Season to taste with salt and pepper.

Ways to Enjoy It

Eat it like John—mix canned white tuna with the Green Goddess Dressing. Stuff the mixture in pita bread and top with chopped iceberg lettuce and grated cheddar cheese. It's also terrific as a dip with poached seafood or crudité.

Flies May Like Walls, but They Hate Cloves

I was an emcee at the Gilroy Garlic Festival, one of my favorite food festivals, when I first noticed halved lemons with cloves stuck in them. I thought they were a simple table decoration, but I learned that they had an important purpose: to keep the flies away.

The reason citronella candles work is because flies do not like the smell of citrus. The winged nuisances also abhor herbs, especially cloves. For a natural, nonchemical solution to the pesky pests, stick several (more is better) whole cloves in half lemons and place them anywhere and everywhere you plan to eat.

I have seen the cloved lemons in action, on a stage with eight cook stations, eight chefs, and countless platters of exposed food, and nary a fly in sight.

This tip is a shoo-in for your next barbecue.

Why Should Martini Drinkers Thank Herb?

Not the plant herb with the silent *h*. Herb the name, as in Herbert Kagley.

In 1933, Herb, a California mechanic, built the prototype for the first mechanical olive pitter. It successfully removed the pits from green olives, leaving the meat intact.

Apparently Herb's motivation wasn't for an easier tapenade; he wanted to enjoy his martini's signature condiment without having to nibble his way around the olive's pit.

Aisle Seven
baked goods, mixes, syrup

A Twenty-Four-Hour Restraining Order for Baking Chocolate Chip Cookies?

In the original *Toll House Cook Book,* published in 1948, Ruth Wakefield revealed that the chocolate chip cookie (originally called chocolate crunch) was an accident. She expected the chips of chocolate to melt into the dough, but was surprised when they remained whole after baking.

She also advised that the dough be chilled overnight prior to baking. Why? Because the extra time in the refrigerator allows the dough to absorb all the liquids, creating a dryer dough. The cold and dry dough bakes and browns more evenly and spreads less. Even though this is a secret many professional bakers have been using for years, the recipe on Toll House's chocolate chip packages doesn't include Wakefield's tip.

I know it's hard not to sample while you're mixing, and even harder to restrain yourself for twenty-four hours before baking, but it's worth the wait!

Breaking Up Is Great to Do!

Have you been shattered when you've broken a favorite piece of pottery?

Wipe your tears. If you save the shards, you can save your brown sugar.

Take a piece of the pottery and soak it in water for 30 minutes. Dry it thoroughly on a paper towel. Add the broken piece to your brown sugar, and it will keep it moist for months.

Batter Up!

When making pancakes with goodies—like chocolate chips or blueberries—don't mix them into the batter. That can change the color of the batter and create a mess.

Instead, prepare your batter and pour it into the pan. As soon as the pancakes start to set on the first side, place your chips or berries on the pancakes. When they settle in, flip the pancakes.

You'll knock them out of the ballpark every time!

A Spoonful of Sugar

Whenever I burn my tongue, I run to the sink. I look like a desperate dog lapping the cool water, but it's soothing.

The tongue is the fastest healing organ in our body, but how do you stop the stinging and smarting without remaining at the sink until it subsides?

Think Mary Poppins. A spoonful of granulated sugar on your tongue will help the stinging go down.

What Is Angel Food Cake's Nemesis?

Devil's food cake.

Just as good guys wear white and bad guys wear black in the movies, those stereotypes are alive and well when it comes to these two cakes. Devil's food—dark, rich, and, as the legend goes, "sinful"—is the counterpoint to angel food sponge cake, which is "heavenly," white, and fluffy.

Angel food cake, often credited as a clever use for leftover egg whites, first appeared in the United States in the 1870s. Devil's food, made with dark chocolate, didn't make its debut until the twentieth century, proving that good guys do come first.

When Is a B Grade Better Than an A Grade?

When it comes to maple syrup.

I used to choose the A, thinking it was the best—it's the top grade, after all—until I read an article Ruth Reichl wrote on *Grub Street San Francisco*. She prefers the dark and robust B, with its intense maple flavor, to the lighter and milder grade A.

Of course it is a matter of taste, but now that I've done my own comparison, I'm a B-syruper all the way. (Plus, I love the lower price.)

No matter what, pure maple syrup of any grade will always beat *maple-flavored syrup*, which contains only a small amount of pure maple syrup, and *pancake syrup*, which typically relies on artificial maple extract or trace amounts of the pure-grade variety.

How Can a Sacrifice Bunt Help You Frost Your Cake?

When a batter bunts the ball to advance one or more runners, he "sacrifices" by getting an out to help his team. The same principle applies when frosting a cake. If you've ever applied the frosting, only to accidentally mix crumbs into it, you might consider a "sacrifice" crumb coat.

My pal Johanna Lasseter-Curtis, owner of Cake Tahoe, taught me her baker's tip.

When the cake is cool, place a thin layer of frosting on all sides. It's okay if some of the crumbs mix in with the frosting—it's going to be sacrificed anyway. Put the cake in the refrigerator and allow the frosting to get cold. When it's fairly hard to the touch, spread on the rest of the frosting with an offset spatula. It should glide over the crumb coat easily. Last, to achieve a professional finish, smooth it with a bench scraper (a basic rectangular baker's tool you can find in any culinary or baking store).

Your cake will be a home run!

Getting a Manicure? Bring the Cooking Spray!

Waiting for your nails to dry following a manicure can be frustrating. If you're like me, you want to save time and smudges. The non-salon solution?

Cooking spray. When your manicure is finished, hold the can several inches away and lightly mist your nails. The cooking spray reacts the same way the quick-dry oils do.

Models have been sharing this secret with each other for years.

Flour Power

Flour is an important baking ingredient, and it can help you with the nitty-gritty too.

Cleaning mushrooms is something I take seriously. There is nothing worse than taking a bite of beautifully cooked mushrooms and chomping on dirt. I have a mushroom brush, but I use it to clean my nails more than my mushrooms. Although I have been advised against using water to clean my mushrooms, I haven't found that it alters the flavor. Further, a bath of flour and water works even better, because the flour acts as an abrasive.

Fill a bowl with cold water and add a handful of flour. Drop the mushrooms in and swirl them around. You will be surprised by the amount of dirt that will immediately float to the top of the water. Remove the mushrooms and drain on a clean dish towel. Polish as needed with a paper towel to remove any remaining specks.

Flour water works great to clean clams too. Or do what Martha Stewart suggests: put cornmeal in the water. The clams will purge sand as they open their lids to feed on the cornmeal.

What Do Duncan Hines and Zagat Have in Common?

Before there was Duncan Hines the cake mix, there was Duncan Hines the restaurant reviewer.

A traveling salesman for years, Hines dined in restaurants across the country and discovered eateries that were off the beaten path and memorable. In 1930, at the age of fifty-five, he began compiling a list of recommended restaurants as a Christmas gift for his friends. Hines started self-publishing his book, *Adventures in Good Eating*, in 1936.

An article in the *Saturday Evening Post* helped solidify Hines as an authority. "Recommended by Duncan Hines" became a seal of approval sought out by hungry American travelers, just like the popular maroon Zagat (rhymes with "the cat") guides that diners rely upon today.

By 1940 Hines had joined forces with Roy Park, and the two created over two hundred and fifty fine food products. Their company merged with Procter & Gamble in 1945, and shortly thereafter the Duncan Hines cake mix was introduced to homemakers.

Duncan Hines knew how to have his cake and eat it, too.

Mouse Cake

Serves 12

My great-grandmother Bessie had a very thick New York accent. Whenever she said Marcy, it sounded like Mossy, which later evolved to Mouse. Only two people still call me by that nickname, my longtime pal Nellsey and my aunt Holly.

1 box Duncan Hines Devil's Food cake mix

1 small package *instant* chocolate pudding mix

¾ cup vegetable oil

¾ cup water

4 eggs

1 (8-ounce) container sour cream

1 (12-ounce) package chocolate chips

Powdered sugar

✤ Preheat the oven to 350°F.

✤ Pour the cake mix and pudding mix into large mixing bowl. Add the vegetable oil, water, eggs, and sour cream. Mix well.

✤ Fold in the chocolate chips.

✤ Pour the batter into a greased and floured 9 × 13-inch or bundt pan. Bake for 50 to 60 minutes.

✤ Dust with powdered sugar after the cake has cooled.

Mouse Cake Variation: Aunt Holly's Favorite

Replace Devil's Food cake mix with a lemon cake mix. Use instant lemon pudding mix instead of instant chocolate pudding mix. Omit the chocolate chips. Create a glaze by mixing lemon juice with powdered sugar, and drizzle over the cooled cake.

A Kernel of Truth About Corn Bread

When adding complementary ingredients to corn bread, such as jalapeno peppers, blueberries, or kernels of corn, flour them before adding them to the batter.

The flour coating allows them to be suspended throughout the batter, rather than fall to the bottom, while baking.

Feb Is More Than Shorthand for February

It is also a reminder of the best order for breading food:

>First: **F**lour
>Second: **E**gg wash
>Third: **B**readcrumbs

It is important to always start with dry ingredients before breading. If you are using salt or seasonings, do it first.

Once you've finished all three steps and an item is breaded, it can wait up to 1 hour before cooking. But never stop at the flour step, or it will become gummy.

If you are going to freeze after breading, be sure that it's still frozen when it is time to cook it. If you defrost it first, the moisture will turn the breading into a mushy mess.

These simple tips should help you any day of the month.

Dor-Eat-Os

Serves 4

I have a thing for onion rings. In this recipe, Doritos provide the lip-smacking crunchy coating. I use Nacho Cheese, but feel free to experiment with other Doritos flavors such as Cool Ranch, Salsa Verde, or Smoky Chipotle BBQ. The rings are baked instead of fried to take the edge off the calorie count. Thank you, Chef D, for the inspiration!

½ cup flour

½ teaspoon baking powder

3 eggs

½ cup milk

3 cups hand-crushed Doritos Nacho Cheese chips

1 large yellow onion, cut into ½-inch slices and rings separated

✣ Preheat the oven to 400°F.

✣ Mix the flour and baking powder. Spread on a large shallow plate.

✣ Whisk the eggs and milk in a bowl.

✣ Using a food processor, pulse the Doritos until they are the consistency of breadcrumbs. Place on a large shallow plate.

✣ Arrange the dishes in the proper breading order: Flour mixture first, egg wash second, and Dorito breading last.

✣ One by one, dip the onion rings in flour until well coated on both sides. Shake off the excess flour, then dip the rings in the egg wash, taking care that the onion is entirely covered. Shake off the excess liquid. Place the onion rings in the Doritos. Turn them several times to coat evenly and thoroughly. Gently lift the Dor-Eat-Os by the sides and place on the sheet pan lined with foil or parchment. It will take two sheet pans or two batches to prepare all the onion rings.

✣ Bake for 20 minutes, rotating halfway through.

✣ Season with additional salt to taste, and serve hot.

POSTSCRIPT

Ketchup is the go-to sauce with rings, but have fun with the dips: ranch dressing with Ranch Dor-Eat-Os, sour cream and onion with the Smoky Chipotle version, or warm bean dip with the Salsa Verde option.

What Can a Swarm of Bees Teach You About Making Custard?

It is difficult to know when custard is finished baking. Inserting a knife into the center is an option, but that leaves an unsightly scar.

Or you can learn to judge by how it moves. If the custard moves in several directions when you gently jiggle the baking dish, it needs more time. When it moves as a mass, all as one, just like a swarm of bees, then it is ready.

Monkeys and Macaroons

They have a lot more in common than *M.*

Cocos nucifera is the scientific name for coconut. *Nucifera* means "nut bearing," but the fun is in the *coco.*

Portuguese seamen in the late fifteenth century observed that the fruit had a hairy shell and three "eyes" (indentations). They named it *coco,* the Spanish word for "monkey face," since it resembled the primate.

When choosing a fresh coconut, be sure it is heavy, that the eyes are dry, and you hear liquid sloshing around when you shake it.

Since most of us aren't going to go to the trouble to shred our own, here are a few things to know about packaged coconut. After you open the bag, store it in the refrigerator or freezer, not the pantry. If it has gone a bit stale, you can restore moisture by steaming it over boiling water or soaking it briefly in milk. If you have rehydrated your coconut, use it all, as it should not be saved for future use.

Monkey-Face Macaroons

25 to 30 cookies

I probably shouldn't monkey around with this classic treat, but I couldn't resist adding currants to give these cookies an enhanced tropical flavor.

1 (7-ounce) package sweetened and shredded coconut

½ cup coconut milk

⅓ cup sugar

2 tablespoons flour

½ teaspoon vanilla

¼ cup currants

2 egg whites

✤ Preheat the oven to 325°F.

✤ In a medium bowl, mix the coconut, coconut milk, sugar, flour, and vanilla. Stir in the currants. In a separate (clean) bowl, beat egg whites until firm and forming peaks. Gently fold the egg whites into the coconut mixture.

✤ Drop by teaspoonfuls, at least 1 inch apart, on a greased or parchment-lined baking sheet. Bake 30 minutes or until lightly browned on top. Cool on a rack.

Jam Versus Jelly

They look alike, they kind of sound alike, but they are not the same. Jam is made from fruit. Jelly is made from fruit juice. Both use sugar and sometimes pectin.

If you find yourself on a cooking reality show, and your challenge is to determine which of two unlabeled jars is jam and which is jelly, you may not want to rely on your taste buds alone. Jam, when turned out of its container, will settle down into a blob. Jelly, on the other hand, will retain its shape.

Marmalade is easier to spot, as it contains pieces of rind.

Preserves are just that. There are medium to large preserved pieces of fruit in the final product, and it can be preserved a long time.

Aisle Eight
soups and sauces

Stock Versus Broth

Consommés are clear, but the difference between stock and broth is not.

Some of the most heated discussions I have had about food, with chefs and home cooks, is the difference between a stock and a broth.

My take: Stock is made with bones. Broth is made with meat. Both are typically cooked with vegetables. Stocks become gelatinous when refrigerated. That's because of the collagen in the bones. Broth, made with meat only and no bones, remains liquid when chilled.

For an expert opinion I refer to the Culinary Institute of America's tome *The Professional Chef*. It explains that broths can be eaten as is, while stocks are part of other dishes.

Most pros agree that there is little difference between canned stock and broth; they can be used interchangeably.

What Does James Bond Know About Making Sauce?

James Bond had several dangerous liaisons, and "liaison" is also the term for a thickening agent, or a mixture that enriches and slightly thickens soups and sauces.

Liaisons are made of egg yolk and cream. Unlike 007's martini, sauces are stirred, not shaken.

Interestingly, the word "liaison" derives from the French word for "bond."

The Eyes Have It!

According to Dr. Brian Wansink's *Mindless Eating*, people use their eyes to count calories, not their stomachs.

He proved it with soup. In his study, participants were randomly assigned to two groups. The first group ate an average portion of soup in a regular bowl. The second group ate from an ingenious refilling bowl, which slowly and imperceptibly kept the bowl constantly full. They consumed a whopping 73 percent more soup, they didn't think they had consumed any more than the participants in the first group, and they weren't any fuller.

Dr. Wansink concluded that "people use their eyes to count calories and not their stomachs." The answer is simple: *mindful* eating rather than *mindless* eating. Use your stomach to determine when you're full, not the amount left in your bowl or on your plate.

That's souper science!

How Can Moses Help You Make the Perfect Reduction Sauce?

The secret of a great reduction sauce is knowing when the sauce is ready. The culinary term for determining this is *nappe*, or when the sauce coats the back of a spoon.

I prefer to take a lesson from Moses in judging when the sauce is properly reduced. When you think your sauce is close to being finished, put a dollop on a clean surface or a plate. Run your finger in a line through the middle of the sauce. If it flows back together, the sauce needs more time to reduce. If it stays on either side of the indentation, er, if the Red Sea stays parted, then you know your reduction sauce is ready.

Thou shalt not serve thy sauce too thick or too thin.

Mint Julep's Silent Partner

The mint julep isn't the only tradition on Kentucky Derby day. There is also Burgoo, a thick soup that's a kissing cousin of Brunswick Stew and nearly as iconic as the mint julep on the first Saturday in May. It's been around for hundreds of years, with as many recipe variations and myths as gumbo or chili.

In the Southern states, Burgoo isn't served exclusively during the Run for the Roses; it is also a side dish for barbecue.

No one knows exactly how Burgoo got its fun name. However, my favorite theory speculates that Burgoo's name is a hybrid of "barbecue" and the French word for a highly seasoned stew, "ragout."

Burgoo is so beloved in the Bluegrass State that a thoroughbred was named Burgoo King. Wearing the lucky number 13, Burgoo King beat the favorites and won the Kentucky Derby in 1932. If you're a sports trivia nut like me, you should know that Burgoo King was the first horse to wear the Blanket of Roses in the winner's circle.

Sonoma Burgoo

Serves 10 to 12

In a tribute to Kentucky and Burgoo's roots, I've included many of the traditional ingredients. I've also added a Sonoma influence—wine! Burgoo can be cooked as long as 12 to 24 hours, but this version cooks in about 3. It's terrific for large gatherings. Serve the same wine you used in the recipe, and don't forget the mint juleps!

2 tablespoons olive oil, plus more for veggies

1½ pounds bone-in pork shoulder

1 pound beef chuck stew meat, cut into 1-inch pieces

1 cup flour

Salt and freshly ground pepper

4 cups beef stock

1 onion, thinly sliced

6 garlic cloves, minced

1 cup hearty red wine

2 cups mini carrots

1 pound Yukon Gold potatoes, cut into 1-inch cubes

2 tablespoons tomato paste

2 cups green beans, trimmed into bite-size pieces

2 ears of corn, kernels only

2 cups rotisserie chicken, shredded

- In Dutch oven or heavy pan, heat the olive oil over medium heat. Dredge the pork shoulder in flour and season with salt and pepper. Brown it on both sides, then remove and set it aside. Dredge the stew meat in flour, season with salt and pepper, and brown it on all sides. Remove and set aside.

- Reduce heat to low and add the onion. Cook 4 minutes or until softened. Add the garlic and cook until aromatic, about 2 minutes. Add the wine to deglaze pan, scraping the delicious bits of meat as you go. Simmer 5 minutes. Add the stock and bring the mixture back to a simmer. Return the pork and beef to pan. Cover and simmer for 2 hours, stirring occasionally.

- Meanwhile, *roast* the root veggies. Preheat the oven to 400°F. Place the carrots and potatoes on a sheet pan. Lightly coat them with olive oil. Roast 30 minutes, turning the veggies once halfway through. Set aside.

- When the Burgoo has cooked 2 hours, turn off the heat. Remove the pork from the soup and cut it into bite-size pieces, discarding bones and fat. Set aside.

- Stir the tomato paste into the soup. Add the pork, carrots, potatoes, green beans, corn, and chicken to pot. Return to a simmer and cook uncovered 1 hour.

- Season with salt and pepper. Ladle into bowls and serve hot.

POSTSCRIPT

I like to serve Burgoo with bottles of Tabasco and Worcestershire on the table or buffet. It's fine to keep cooking the Burgoo for more than 3 hours. It will get thicker and thicker, the longer it goes. Some Burgoo enthusiasts insist it isn't Burgoo unless the spoon stands upright in it.

Hollandaise Versus Béarnaise

Both hollandaise and béarnaise are emulsion sauces made of a vinegar or wine reduction, butter, and egg yolks.

Hollandaise is flavored with lemon juice and typically served with eggs, vegetables, and fish. Béarnaise is finished with tarragon and chervil and most often served with meat.

What Can Dancing with the Stars Teach You About Pasta Sauce?

The quick step is popular on the ballroom floor, and quick sauce is popular in Italy.

I used to think that a really great tomato sauce simmered for a long time, but that's not always true. Tomato sauce that has been cooked a long time will have more concentrated flavors, but quick sauces are fresh and vibrant.

It's no jive that you can hustle a terrific tomato sauce in just 20 minutes.

Smooshed Sauce

Serves 4

This is a hands-on recipe, meaning you must get your hands on the tomatoes! I was first taught the smoosh technique in Benevento, the homeland of my grandfather. Chef Arturo Iengo of Ristorante Pascalucci was explaining how he made his tomato sauce. It was all in Italian, so I missed most of it, but there was no missing the smoosh technique. Italians talk with their hands and apparently they cook with them, too.

2 tablespoons olive oil

2 tablespoons butter

½ cup onion, minced

4 cloves of garlic, thinly sliced

1½ teaspoons salt, or more to taste

1 (28-ounce) can San Marzano tomatoes (DOP, imported from Italy preferred)

1 Parmigiano-Reggiano cheese rind, if available (see "What Do Ab Exercises and a Famous Italian Cheese Have in Common?," page 57)

✤ Melt the butter and olive oil in a 3-quart saucepan. (You'll want the extra room in the larger pan to act as a splashguard when it's smoosh time.)

✤ When the oil is warm and the butter is melted, add the onions. Cook 4 to 5 minutes or until softened. Add the garlic and salt and continue cooking 2 to 3 minutes. Add the juices of the tomatoes to the saucepan and mix with onions and garlic.

✤ Smoosh the tomatoes with your hands over the saucepan, making sure they are broken into small pieces. Mix the sauce together and add the cheese rind. Simmer uncovered for 20 to 30 minutes. Adjust for salt before serving.

POSTSCRIPT

Some scoff at using both onion and garlic in their tomato sauce, but I do, because I can't choose just one. Feel free to let the Smooshed Sauce keep cooking on a low simmer. It will get thicker and richer.

Making a Tastier Tomato Sauce with Canned Tomatoes

There is nothing like tomatoes from your garden, but when it comes to making red sauce, please don't look askance at canned tomatoes. When packaged correctly, they are picked at the peak of their freshness and preserved immediately to maintain flavor.

Although there are countless varieties, cuts, and preparations, you should know about San Marzanos, especially if you are making a tomato-based sauce.

San Marzano tomatoes, often the preferred tomato in Italian recipes and similar to Romas, can be grown anywhere. However, those grown in the volcanic soil near Mt. Vesuvius in Campania, and certified DOP (translated PDO in English) are in a category all their own.

DOP stands for Protected Designation of Origin. That means that the product was grown or made in a designated geographic region, under strict standards, ensuring the highest quality. Don't be duped by a photo or illustration of a San Marzano on the label; look for DOP on the label.

I have evaluated the color, texture, and taste of domestic canned tomatoes against the DOP varieties from Italy, and in my mind, there is no comparison.

Bunkbeds and Sauces

I remember fierce rounds of roshambo to win the top bunk. Camp was never fun if you were stuck sleeping on the bottom bunk.

When it comes to saucing, foods have their own preferences for top or bottom too.

Moist preparations, such as poaching or steaming, like to have their sauces placed on top, because food cooked in liquid tends to appear bland. The sauce makes it pretty.

For dry heat preparations, such as roasting or grilling, the sauce should be on the bottom, the better to show off the color and texture of the food.

How Can the NFL Help You with Your Braises?

By understanding the importance of "offsides."

In football the term refers to the foul for being across the line of scrimmage before the ball is snapped. Off-sides should also be part of your braising technique.

Braising is typically done in the oven, with liquid, in a covered pot. When checking your braise to turn the meat or adjust the liquid, be sure to scrape the sides of the pot clean. If you fail to get the food off the sides, it will burn, and the chunks will fall in the pot, altering the flavor of the sauce.

That's a fumble that is hard to recover.

Does It Really Have to Be Said Twice?

A minor pet peeve here. Please indulge me.

Au jus is a French phrase that means "with juice." *Au* means "with," and *jus* means "juice."

So why do many restaurant menus list "roast beef *with* au jus"? That's redundant. It's the same as saying "roast beef with with juice."

I have never seen "café with au lait" listed on coffee-house menus.

Au revoir to poor food grammar.

Mother Sauces Have Nothing to Do with Your Mom

In the nineteenth century, Marie-Antoine Carême, whom many consider the father of French cuisine, developed the classification of the four basic sauces. He called them "mother sauces," because they are the basis, give birth to, if you will, an array of variations. Later in the twentieth century, Auguste Escoffier redefined them and added a fifth.

Are they important to know? If you're seriously interested in cooking, I think so. Even if you can't make them, it's good to be able to list them. A pal of mine auditioned for a popular television show featuring home cooks, and when she couldn't list the five mother sauces, she was sent home.

Simplified, the mother (also known as grand) sauces are béchamel (white sauce made with milk and thickened with a pale roux), velouté (white stock thickened with a white roux), espagnole (brown sauce made with brown stock and thickened with a brown roux), hollandaise, and tomato sauce.

Their offspring include bordelaise, mornay, and good ol' gravy.

Roux of Thumb

When you are making a roux, the classic concoction of flour and fat to thicken a sauce, soup, or stew, use your nose, not just your eyes, to determine when to stop cooking it.

For a white roux, when it stops smelling like starch, it is done. Once it begins to smell like nuts, the roux is on its way to becoming blond. When a roux is cooked all the way to brown, the nutty aroma will have intensified and smell like slightly burned toast.

The brown roux will also have less thickening power, because the longer it cooks, the more the starches in the flour break down, making it harder for the roux to do its job of thickening. It's a simple roux-le: the darker the roux, the more intense the flavor and the more roux you will need.

Lumps? It's fairly easy to avoid them if you remember that opposites attract. Add cool roux to hot liquid and cool liquid to hot roux. (Warm liquid may be added to warm roux.) No matter what, avoid extremely hot and cold temperatures altogether, as they will roux-in your efforts every time.

Is That Michael Phelps Swimming in Your Bowl?

Phelps may have been called a fish since his first days in the pool. However, I doubt he'd fit in the bowl as easily as a crustacean.

The French word *nage,* which means "swimming," is a preparation in which seafood is poached in stock or court bouillon (broth with vegetables and herbs). Think of *nage* as cooked fish swimming in soup.

When a dish *à la nage* is served to you, it will typically be seafood in a bowl, surrounded with broth and garnished with julienned vegetables. Deep-ending on the whim of the chef, the broth may be poured tableside.

Be sure to make a splash with your pals by pronouncing "nahj" correctly.

Sonofabitch Stew

I was looking for sorghum in Alan Davidson's *The Oxford Companion to Food,* when I noticed the entry preceding it. It was for Sonofabitch Stew, and I did a double take.

It's not that I like to curse, but I was intrigued by the name enough to learn that it is a cowboy dish made primarily from the organs of a freshly killed calf. There is a specific order in which the ingredients are added, the toughest pieces first and the brain last. That may be because gray matter is very tender and cooks quickly.

Back in the day, the name was adapted for anyone unpopular at the time. Cleveland Stew was coined by cattlemen for the president, as in Grover, who gave away the land the buckaroos had leased from the Cherokees.

Perhaps I should break out the Dutch oven and rustle up some Bernie Madoff Stew?

The King's Sauce

Pleasing a king is no small matter. Only the best is presented to the royal table. Henderson William Brand, chef to England's King George IV, created a special sauce for the king in the early nineteenth century. The king was impressed with the sauce and dubbed it "A1."

Chef Brand left the palace to pursue his culinary career. Perhaps he should have thought more carefully about his job security behind the moat, because although he was a master chef, his business manufacturing meat extracts and essences failed years later, reducing him to pauper status.

A1 sauce was so good, though, it survived ownership changes and legal battles in the ensuing years. The sauce was trademarked "A1 Steak Sauce" by Dence and Mason.

We, the loyal subjects, are still enjoying the king's sauce today.

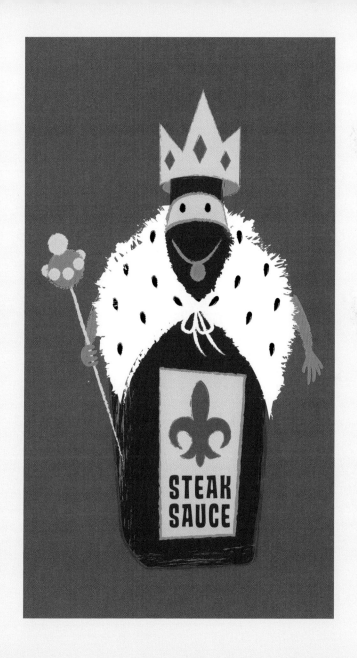

King's Steak

Serves 4 to 6

I've loved A1 steak sauce since I was a kid. Whoever says putting it on a steak is like putting ketchup on steak is a sauce snob in my book. A1 is more than a dipping sauce; it works well in a marinade too. This dish is tangy, thanks to the mustard and lemon, and lean, thanks to the low-fat cut.

2 pounds flank steak

Garlic salt (I use Lawry's Garlic Salt Coarse Ground with Parsley)

¾ cup A1 Steak Sauce

2 tablespoons French's yellow mustard

1 tablespoon Worcestershire sauce

1 tablespoon lemon juice

✤ Sprinkle garlic salt generously on both sides of the flank steak. Mix the A1 Sauce, mustard, Worcestershire, and lemon juice. Spread the marinade on both sides of the flank steak. Place the steak in a 1-gallon resealable bag or nonreactive dish. Marinate in refrigerator for 2 to 3 hours, turning the bag over every 30 minutes or so. (Be sure and remove the steak from fridge 20 minutes before cooking—you don't want to start with cold meat.)

✤ Heat a grill to high or the oven to broil (the rack should be in the top third of the oven). Cook until desired doneness.

✤ Allow the steak to rest 10 minutes. Slice it diagonally across the grain and serve warm.

Variation: King's Roll-Ups

King's Steak can abdicate and become King's Roll-Ups. Slice the flank steak in 1 × 5-inch pieces. Place a mini dill pickle or cornichon in the center of each piece, roll up, and secure with a toothpick.

Are You Fond of Fond?

When I was first learning about pan sauces, I was a bit confused. I thought I heard my instructor say, "Save the fawn." I was baffled about what Bambi was doing in our cooking demo. Embarrassed, I raised my hand and was corrected. *Fond* is a French term for stock. It also means the pan drippings remaining after sautéing or roasting food.

So save the fond!

Don't scrub pan drippings out of your pan—save those little tasty bits and caramelized crunchies. Instead of taking your pan to the sink, keep it on the stove. Add stock, wine, or other liquid to deglaze the pan, and you'll have the base of a sauce I know you'll be fond of.

Aisle Nine
pasta and rice

To Oil or Not to Oil? That Is the Question . . .

Does oil in the water keep pasta from sticking?

It's the volume of water that you cook your pasta in that's most important. Don't crowd your pasta when you're cooking it—give it room! Pasta should be cooked in 4 to 5 quarts of water per pound of noodles.

To further prevent sticking, yes, a small amount of oil is helpful, as is constantly stirring the pasta the *first few minutes* after it hits the boiling water.

If you give your pasta plenty of space to toss and tumble, it will be the nobler deed.

Why Should You Give Rice the Finger?

Making rice can be intimidating. There's a simple technique that works every time whether you are making 1 cup of rice or 5.

Rinse short-grain rice to remove the excess starch. Long-grain rice does not need to be rinsed. Place the rice in the pot. Now your finger can do the rest.

If you are making short-grain rice, measure the water from the top of the rice to the top of your thumbnail. If you are making long-grain rice, measure the water from the top of the rice to the top of your first knuckle. Cover and cook.

I'm not sure why this fail-safe formula is magic. It must be presto *digit-ation*!

Bo's Fried Rice

Serves 4 to 6
as a side dish

I took my son, Bo, to China when he was in the sixth grade. We had a contest to see who would give in and eat Western food first. I lost. Bo's staple was fried rice. It's meant to be made with leftover rice, so plan accordingly. If you are making it for dinner tonight, make the rice as soon as possible, as it must be cold. For the char siu, I've never had success making it at home, so I buy an appetizer portion of sliced BBQ pork from my local Chinese restaurant.

1 tablespoon oil

¼ cup minced onions

2 eggs, lightly beaten

4 cups cooked long-grain rice, cold and best a day old

1 tablespoon soy sauce

1 tablespoon oyster sauce

1 cup *defrosted* frozen peas and carrots

1 cup BBQ pork, about 8 ounces, cut into ¼-inch dice

2 green onions, thinly sliced

✤ Heat the oil in large skillet or wok. Be sure the cooking surface is completely coated.

✤ When the oil is hot, add the onions. Sauté them quickly until they are lightly browned, about 1 minute. Add the eggs and stir frequently until they are starting to set, about 30 seconds. Add the rice and mix it well with the onion and eggs, about 3 minutes. Add the soy sauce and oyster sauce, constantly moving the rice to blend and evenly color it. Add the carrots and peas, stirring all the time, about 3 minutes. Add the pork and continue stir-frying, about 1 minute.

✤ Serve on a warm platter and sprinkle green onions on top.

Meat and Vegetarian Options

The Chinese often use sausage in their fried rice, so if you can't get BBQ pork, use Aidells' chicken and apple sausage or Aidells' pineapple and bacon sausage. Oyster sauce is readily available in the Asian section of supermarkets, but if you are omitting the pork to make a vegetarian version, look for "vegetable" oyster sauce, which is available at Asian stores and online.

What Does Oscar Wilde Know About French Cooking?

Oscar Wilde wrote the farce *The Importance of Being Earnest*.

Farce (pronounced "far-say") is also the French cooking term for stuffing.

Farce's not the type of traditional stuffing we associate with Thanksgiving. Also known as forcemeat, it's comprised of fish, meat, chicken, or vegetables.

Should You Throw Your Rice?

We've all seen the newlyweds showered in rice, but there is another reason to throw your rice—at least in India.

Chinese rice is often served sticky. Indians, however, serve their rice dry.

Chef Mark Ainsworth, Culinary Institute of America professor, learned this in India. Toss a handful of cooked basmati rice across the counter. If it is prepared properly, it will scatter and separate.

Should You Go Skin-Ny Dipping with Your Pasta?

Yes, if you want to try a delicious Italian dish, but before you get your bikini on, read further.

Gnudi means "nude" in Italian. Akin to a boiled dumpling, gnudis are skinless. Think ravioli without the pasta.

Just because you don't see the dough on the outside, gnudis are not necessarily carb or gluten free; most recipes call for flour or breadcrumbs as a binder.

As far as I know, there are no gnudi colonies in Italy.

Gnudis à la Marcellina

Serves 4 as main course or 8 as appetizer

I was in San Gusme, a seven-hundred-year-old walled village in Chianti, when I first tried gnudis. I had already been traveling in Italy for a week and was drawn to the lighter pasta. Beg as I may (maybe it was my inept Italian?), I did not come home with the recipe. I did my best to re-create it here.

1 (15-ounce) container ricotta cheese

¾ cup steamed spinach, squeezed dry and chopped

2 tablespoons chopped sun-dried tomatoes (not oil-packed)

2 tablespoons flour, plus more to coat

⅓ cup unflavored bread-crumbs

2 teaspoons salt

2 egg yolks

✣ Place the ricotta in a large bowl. Add the spinach and sun-dried tomatoes. Add the flour, bread-crumbs, salt, and egg yolks. Mix to combine. Mold the mixture into small ¾-inch balls. Roll the balls lightly in flour to coat.

✣ Drop the balls into salted, briskly simmering water (if the water is at a full boil the gnudis can break apart). Cook 3 to 4 minutes, or until the balls rise to the top.

✣ Serve with my Smooshed Sauce (page 141), a prepared red sauce, or brown butter.

Slip and Slide

Concerned about the sticky clump of pasta in your colander after cooking it? Should you rinse it? I don't, unless directed by a recipe.

If you rinse it, some of the surface starches will go down the drain with the water, making it slippery. The sauce will tend to slide off. If you skip the rinsing, the starches on the pasta will help the sauce cling.

There is an Italian saying, "Pasta waits for no one." So don't make your pasta wait. Have everything ready before you drop the pasta in the boiling water. Don't allow it to sit in the colander more than a minute before tossing it with sauce and serving it.

If you must rinse it, and I know a lot of you must, use the cooking water. (Remove several cups from the pot before draining it.) It won't cook the pasta any further, it will prevent the pasta from sticking, and it will keep the pasta warm until you get around to serving it.

If you are going to serve the pasta cold or are cooking noodles you have to handle with your hands, like lasagna, then rinsing the pasta in cool water is fine.

What Do a Coroner and the Clean-Plate Club Have in Common?

The heroine in many of Patricia Cornwell's bestselling books is Chief Medical Examiner Kay Scarpetta.

Scarpetta is also the Italian term for cleaning your plate with a piece of bread. No need to waste that tasty bolognese or clam sauce. Scoop it up and enjoy.

One cadaver, er, caveat: *scarpetta* is only acceptable at home or in a casual restaurant while dining in Italy.

Instant Success?

When Momofuku Ando invented a ramen that could be ready in minutes, you'd think his instant noodles would have been an instant success.

Introduced in Japan in 1958, Ando's chicken ramen was initially rejected by consumers. With fresh udon noodles available in markets for a fraction of the price, the instant ramen was considered a luxury item.

It took a full year, but the chicken ramen eventually caught on with the public. Ten companies began manufacturing their version of instant noodles, and grocery stores couldn't stock enough.

Today Top Ramen and Cup Noodles are still owned by Nissin Foods, the company that Ando founded. No, that's not a typo. It is Cup Noodles. Originally named Cup O' Noodles, the "O" was dropped in 1993.

Should You Surf with Your Risotto?

A well-prepared risotto should not be firm and stiff. It should be soft and creamy, or *all'onda*, the Italian term for "wavelike."

Rice that is covered and left alone to cook is not risotto. To be a true risotto, the rice, typically arborio, must be stirred and cooked in an open pot. Liquid is added in batches—some evaporates and some is absorbed by the rice, until the desired tenderness and *all'onda* are achieved.

Making your risotto wavy will have your guests shouting, "Cowabunga!"

How Can You Save Calories When Cooking Pasta?

Did you notice that I asked how to save calories when cooking, not eating, pasta?

Everyone knows that light, olive-oil based sauces are less fattening than heavy, cream-based sauces, but did you know that cooking your pasta *al dente* ("to the tooth" in Italian, or with a firm bite) can save you calories?

That's because the slightly undercooked pasta has a lower glycemic index than pasta that has been cooked to soft or mushy. Translation: You may get fuller faster and the lower glycemic index helps stabilize your blood sugar levels. And don't be fooled by the cooking times on the package. Set the timer for a few minutes less than recommended.

As carb conscious as I am, life's too short to forgo pasta. I always eat it al dente, but now I can smile about it.

What Can a Volcano Teach You About Making Polenta?

When making polenta, it can be difficult to know when it is finished cooking.

Think of lava erupting from a volcano. The finished polenta should have the same oozing consistency as hot lava running down the side of a volcano.

Should You Cook Your Pasta in Ocean Water?

Ocean water is salty, and the cooking water for pasta should be salty too. The amount may surprise you. I don't mean a sprinkle or two from the shaker. For every six quarts of water, add 1½ ounces (3 tablespoons) of kosher salt.

If you're in the habit of adding the salt to the water before the water is boiled, do as Willie Wonka says, "Strike that, reverse it, thank you." Add the salt *after* the water has started boiling. It's about flavor, not about making the water boil faster.

If you're still shaking your head, salt doesn't make water boil faster at all. Harold McGee, author of *On Food and Cooking*, advises that to match the salinity of the ocean, literally, you need to add 1 ounce of salt for every quart of water. Even then, it will only raise the boiling point by one degree.

PASTA
AND RICE

Rice Rules

Even though I live in America, I still try to adapt to and honor the tradition of the cuisine I am eating. When it comes to Asian food, one of my favorites, there are a few customs to consider.

Sushi means "vinegar-seasoned rice." Sushi is a category of menu items that use vinegar-seasoned rice combined with fish and vegetables. For *nigiri* sushi, hand-formed bricks of rice are topped with slices of raw fish. For *makimono* ("rolls"), a sheet of sushi is topped with fillings, rolled up, and sliced into cylindrical pieces. *Temaki* is a cone-shaped hand roll. *Sashimi* is raw meat or fish thinly sliced and served by itself.

In a Japanese restaurant, don't dip the rice of your nigiri in the soy sauce. Turn it over and dip the fish side only. It is customary to eat it in one bite. And don't worry, it's perfectly acceptable to eat your nigiri with your hands if you're not adept with chopsticks.

It is poor etiquette to leave rice on the *geta* ("get-tah"), the raised wooden platform on which your food is served. I learned this when I used to pick off excess rice from the bottom of my nigiri or out of my temaki hand rolls. Although it all was in an effort to save carbs and calories, I was advised by a sushi chef to leave the *geta* clean and never messy. To circumvent the breach and save myself from hiding the leftover rice in a paper napkin on my lap, I now order my nigiri with half rice and my temaki with no rice and triple veggies.

When eating rice from a bowl, the Japanese bring the chopsticks from the bowl up to their mouth, much like we do with a fork and plate. Only when it gets down to the last grains of rice do they bring the bowl to their lips to finish it.

The Chinese may be famous for their acrobats, but they do not try to perform a balancing act when eating rice. They start and finish with the bowl positioned at their lips, so they can scoop the rice into their mouths.

Both cultures are superstitious about leaving chopsticks upright in the rice bowl. The reasons vary, all having to do with respecting the dead and funerals, so to be safe, always lay them horizontally along the rim of the rice bowl.

Finally, both the Chinese and the Japanese like their steamed rice pristine; they do not add soy sauce to it.

BLT Sushi

12 pieces

When I was taking a skill development class at the Culinary Institute of America, I walked past a tray full of sashimi-size pieces of pristine raw tuna. Or so I thought. It was actually peeled Roma tomatoes cut in quarters. I was so taken aback by how similar the two looked, I decided to create a canapé with them. Traditional sushi rice recipes call for rice wine vinegar, sugar, and salt. I keep it plain here so as not to overwhelm the traditional BLT flavors. It is important to use short-grain rice, sometimes labeled sushi rice. Long-grain won't do. Be sure to rinse it at least two times before cooking.

1 cup cooked sushi rice

3 Roma tomatoes

3 slices cooked bacon

12 pieces spring or romaine lettuce cut in 2-inch rectangles

Sea salt

If you've ever seen nigiri sushi, you'll know how to mimic the appearance. Measurements are approximate. Have fun!

✤ Prepare Roma tomatoes with the "X Marks the Spot" technique (see page 33). Seed and cut them into quarters. Trim the edges so that each piece is the size of the fish slice typically used on nigiri, a rectangle, about 3 inches long and 1 inch wide.

✤ Cut the bacon slices into four even pieces.

✤ While the rice is still warm, mold it into twelve 2-inch bricks. Be careful not to pack the rice too tightly, or it will break and become mushy.

✤ Place a lettuce leaf on top of each brick of rice. Top each with a piece of bacon and then a slice of tomato.

✤ Lightly season the tomato with sea salt to taste.

POSTSCRIPT
If you can't resist the urge to dip—even though this is bacon and not fish—go ahead and serve soy sauce or a spicy mayonnaise.

wine,
beer,
spirits

What Does Champagne Do If It's Fourth and Ten?

Punt.

Every champagne bottle has one, as do many other sparkling wines. The punt is the inverted dome at the bottom of the bottle. Its purpose is to reinforce the bottle and strengthen it, especially in champagne bottles, which contain tremendous pressure.

Although it is not always an indication of quality, having a punt in the bottle generally tells you that the champagne is a higher caliber wine. The punt is necessary for any champagne produced with *méthode champenoise,* the oldest and most traditional way to make sparkling wine, in which the secondary fermentation takes place in a sealed bottle.

Proseccos and Astis, for example, are made in a less complex manner, with their secondary fermentations done in bulk tanks. These tasty wines, which are lighter than champagne, are found in bottles with or without punts.

What Can Black Mold Teach You About Whiskey?

During Prohibition, police were always on the lookout for moonshine operations in the back hills of Tennessee. The bootleggers were cunning and hid their amateur distilleries deep in the woods, cleverly camouflaging the equipment to evade detection. Except there was one thing that gave away their hideouts every time: black mold.

It turns out that ethyl alcohol from fermenting, distilling, and aging whiskey feeds naturally occurring molds. These molds have a voracious appetite, and their favorite food is ethyl alcohol. The ethyl alcohol encourages the molds, and a black fungus develops that is impossible to eradicate.

All the cops had to do was look for trees with black bark and they were sure to find a still nearby. You can still see the same black fungus on the barns of the Jack Daniel Distillery, the oldest operating and licensed distillery in the United States.

Speaking of licensed, although it's legal to make wine and beer at home, it is against the law to distill spirits for personal purposes. (Unless you are approved by the government to be a distilled spirits plant—not likely.)

Jack in the Beans

Serves 6

It's Old No. 7 that is proudly displayed on all Jack Daniel's whiskey labels. In Jack Daniel's 146-year history, there have been only seven master distillers, and Tennessee native Jeff Arnett is the seventh. Jeff introduced me to Lynne Tolley, Jack Daniel's great-grandniece. Lynne graciously shared her seven-ingredient recipe, a tribute to her uncle Jack and his whiskey.

---

2 tablespoons bacon drippings or oil

1 small onion, chopped

2 tablespoons brown sugar

⅓ cup Jack Daniel's Tennessee Whiskey

1 (28-ounce) can baked beans

1 tablespoon spicy brown mustard

2 tablespoons Worcestershire sauce

✤ Heat the drippings or oil in a large saucepan. Stir in the onion and brown sugar. Cook over medium heat, stirring frequently, until the onion is soft and golden brown, about 5 minutes. Stir in the remaining ingredients. Simmer 20 to 30 minutes.

POSTSCRIPT

The next time you're in Lynchburg, Tennessee, be sure and experience Lynne's southern hospitality at Miss Mary BoBo's Boarding House Restaurant. Tell 'em Marcy sent you!

Should You Ask Your Waiter for a Breathalyzer When Ordering Cherries Jubilee?

I can't tell you how many times I told my dinner guests not to worry, that all the alcohol was cooked out of the cherries jubilee. Oops! I was wrong, but at least I was in good company, because many professional chefs are mistaken too.

According to Harold McGee in *On Food and Cooking*, experiments have shown that briefly cooked dishes retain 10 to 50 percent of the alcohol. If you cook two to three hours, such as for a long-simmered stew, you'll be down to about 5 percent.

And your cherries jubilee? After it is flamed, 75 percent of the alcohol remains. So please, eat your dessert responsibly.

What Qualities Do Deodorant and Champagne Share?

Extra Brut, Brut, and Extra Dry.

When it comes to champagne, it's the Extra Dry that is the *sweetest*. Go figure. It has between 12 and 20 grams of sugar per liter. Extra Brut is the *driest*, with less than 6 grams of sugar per liter. Brut falls in the middle with less than 12 grams of sugar per liter.

The sweetest of all are the dessert champagnes, Sec, Demi-Sec, and especially Doux.

As with deodorant, don't sweat the small stuff. Choose the champagne variety that works for you.

Top Shelf Versus Well

Happy Hour menus frequently feature cocktails made with well drinks. Well drinks may infer inexpensive liquor, but they are actually called "well" because that's where the bottles are kept—in the well, a long shelf, underneath the counter.

Top shelf refers to the premium liquor. It is stored on the highest shelves behind the bar in the sight line of the patrons sitting at the bar. That's why the best stuff is referred to as "top shelf."

Raisin D'être

Raisins can revive leftover sparkling wine. Now that's a reason for living!

If you've ever been frustrated by finding your unfinished sparkling wine flat a day later, put a few raisins in the bottle. The uneven surface of the raisins helps the remaining dissolved CO_2 to come out—it's the CO_2, carbon dioxide, that creates the bubbles.

What if you don't have raisins? Then eliminate the need for them entirely and preserve your bubbles correctly from the start. Use a stopper made specifically for champagne, the type that hooks on the edge with wings that wrap around the neck of the bottle. Properly sealing it prevents the CO_2 from escaping. Keep it well chilled—that will also help maintain the CO_2 in the sparkling wine.

Can Vegans Drink Wine?

It's difficult to pair artichokes with wine, but that's not my point.

Some wines are fined. Fining is a process that softens wine and makes it clear by reducing particulates and harsh-tasting substances such as tannins. Most fining

agents are animal-based products such as egg whites, gelatin, casein (a milk by-product), and isinglass (dried fish bladder). Bentonite clay, used for white wine, and silica are exceptions.

It is not a significant amount, and it does not affect taste. However, vegetarian or vegan purists should know that animal by-products might have been used if the wine was fined.

Federal law does not mandate that the fining agent be disclosed, so if unfined wine is important to you, look for it to be listed as such on the label.

In-Season Vegetables, Yes, but What About In-Season Beer?

What is it with those Belgians and yeast? Big, fluffy waffles and fluffy beer too.

Saison means "season" in French, and it's also the name of a style of beer. Invented in the farm country of Belgium over a century ago, it was brewed in the winter with whatever was available, and stored for consumption the following summer. It's akin to a rustic Italian house wine fermented in the basement. Nothing fancy, and meant to be enjoyed every day at home.

In America, Saison is known as farmhouse ale. It has become popular with craft breweries because of its refreshing and easy-drinking style.

What Do Your Car Tire and Champagne Have in Common?

Pressure. There's more pressure in a bottle of champagne than there is in your car tire. The average tire has 30 pounds per square inch of pressure, and there's at least that waiting to explode underneath that champagne cork. Here's how to open it safely every time.

First, remove the foil. Untwist the wire cage, also known as the muselet. If you've been counting, you'll know it will always untwist in six turns. Place the bottle in your strongest hand, cover it with a towel, and tilt it at a forty-five degree angle. Turn the *bottle,* not the cork.

When you serve the champagne, put your thumb in the punt (that's the inverted dome at the bottom of the bottle). Pour along the side of a tilted glass. The bubbles will fizz as the temperature goes from cold in the bottle to warm in the glass. After popping the cork, always keep the champagne bottle on ice.

Harvest in a Glass

Serves 6 to 8

During one of my first harvests living in the wine country, I was served a Chardonnay Bellini at Tra Vigne in St. Helena. Freshly pressed Chardonnay juice replaced the peach puree. It tasted like harvest in a glass—sweet and celebratory. Although it is nearly impossible for home cooks to get Chardonnay grapes, we can buy red seedless grapes year around. They provide the same just-plucked-from-the-vineyard refreshment.

1 pound red seedless grapes

1 bottle chilled champagne or sparkling wine

✤ Wash the grapes, remove them from the stem, and allow the skins to dry.

✤ Put the grapes (skins and all) into a blender or food processor and pulverize them until the fruit is liquefied.

✤ Pour 2 inches of red grape juice into a flute and top with champagne or sparkling wine.

Make a Mocktail

Substitute ginger ale for the champagne or sparkling wine.

She's Got Legs and She Knows How to Use Them

The iconic ZZ Top song can help you sound like a pro when evaluating wine.

You may have heard a wine-o-phile say, "This wine has great legs." But what does that mean?

Legs, a combination of alcohol and water, are the rivulets of wine that appear on the glass after swirling. As the alcohol evaporates, the water trickles down the side of the glass. The higher the alcohol content, the more visible the legs will be.

Don't ooh and ahh over the legs too quickly. The presence or absence of legs is not an indication of quality.

Your Stomach Growls. Can Your Beer Growl Too?

Back in the day, beer was transported from the pub in a pail. Legend has it that as the CO_2 escaped, the beer made a growling noise. Over the years the word "growler" came to signify any container that was used to carry beer home from the brewery.

In modern times, especially with the advent of brewpubs, growlers are glass to-go jugs that hold a half gallon of beer.

The only growling noise associated with beer these days is when it is warm or when it is out.

Som Grape Advice

Sommeliers are the wine experts in restaurants who make recommendations and provide the wine service. They are also known affectionately as "soms."

A master sommelier is part of an elite group with exceptional wine knowledge. Less than two hundred people have received that distinction in the world.

No matter what, please don't be intimidated by sommeliers. Hospitality is their business. A former kitchen cabinet member for *The Food Guy and Marcy Show*, Master Sommelier Evan Goldstein, used to tell our listeners that one of his favorite challenges was finding a reasonable bottle of wine for a table of four where the guests were having disparate meals of fish, chicken, beef, and duck.

It is perfectly acceptable to set a price first, even if you aren't sure what varietal you prefer.

When the wine is presented to you, that's your chance to confirm it's the wine you ordered and the correct vintage. It's not good form to send it back because you noticed it was the wrong bottle or wrong year after it has been opened. It's fine to return a wine that is defective or corked (a musty smell), but that should be just after you tasted it, not after a glass or two have been consumed.

If you are bringing wine in to the restaurant, there are a few rules to follow:

1. Do not bring a bottle that is already on the wine list (unless it is a rare vintage they don't offer). Call ahead to confirm.

2. Be aware of the corkage fee and be prepared to pay it. If you are having a large party, the fee can sometimes be negotiated, but it must be arranged in advance. Some restaurants encourage business by waiving corkage fees on designated nights.

3. For every bottle you bring in, you should buy a bottle from the restaurant.

4. Ask the som if he or she is familiar with the wine. If not, offer a taste.

5. If you can't finish a bottle that you either brought in or purchased, it's a nice gesture to leave it for the staff to taste after service is completed.

Follow these basic guidelines, and you'll be the toast of the restaurant.

Forget About Proof of Purchase. What About Proof of Alcohol?

In the seventeenth and eighteenth centuries, in order to verify that whiskey was indeed whiskey, gunpowder was added to a sample taken from the barrel. A flame was put to the mixture, and if it ignited, that was "proof" that it was alcohol. Distilled spirits that contain more water than alcohol won't burn.

Nowadays alcohol content is measured by the ABV formula, which calculates the percentage of alcohol by volume.

In the United States, understanding alcohol percentage is simple math—it is always half the proof. If the label says 80 proof, it's 40 percent alcohol.

It's Better to Be the Hare Than the Tortoise When It Comes to Pouring Beer

Beer does not like to be poured slowly. It needs agitation to release its aromas and build foam.

Always use a clean glass. And not from the dishwasher. Wash it by hand in hot soapy water, rinse thoroughly and air dry. Residue from other beverages, particles of food that may have shared the dishwasher, even lint from a dish towel, will affect the quality of your pour—the beer's bubbles will cling to the film on the glass, and the bubbles in the foam head will collapse faster.

Begin pouring with the glass at a forty five degree angle. When the glass is half full, bring the glass upright and finish pouring into the middle of the glass. Alternately, you can pour until the head is about 2 inches deep, stop and wait until the head recedes, then top it off.

When it is time to quaff, that's when it's better to be the tortoise than the hare. Drink slowly and drink responsibly.

Is There a Pony in Your Peach Daiquiri?

Most likely, yes, but not the small breed of horse that kids ride at birthday parties.

Early cocktail measures utilized common glassware. A pony was a 1½-ounce stemmed liquor glass for cordials. These days a pony usually refers to the measurement of 1 ounce of liquor, or what we typically refer to as a shot.

If you're curious what the mane difference is between a pony and a jigger, I'll fill you in a bit. A jigger originated in its heyday as a 1¼-ounce shot glass. It later evolved into the two-ended tool we know today, with one end holding 1½ ounces, and the other end ¾ ounce.

This information should help you the next time you saddle up to the bar.

A Bloody Good Punch

Sangria is one of the world's most popular punches. It derives from the traditional red wine punch made throughout Europe, which may explain how it got its name, because, translated, *sangria* means "blood." Red wine was the main ingredient, but brandy and fruit were added later to pack more punch in the punch.

Spain made sangria famous, but Americans became familiar with it after sangria was served at the 1964 World's Fair in New York.

Although there is no official recipe for Sangria, the key ingredients are wine, sliced fruit (usually citrus), fruit juice, and a bit of brandy, gin, or vodka. If you're looking for some bubbles, use sparkling water or soda.

Don't confuse sangria with sangrita. They are two entirely different concoctions. Sangria originated in Spain, and sangrita hails from Mexico.

Spirits expert Steve Beal (whom I call my spiritual adviser, since he is also a pastor) explained on *The Food Guy and Marcy Show* that sangrita was created to quench the fire of homemade tequila and soon became a Mexican tradition. It is a concoction that includes tomatoes, orange juice, lime juice, onions, salt, and hot chili peppers. It is often enjoyed as a chaser after a shot of tequila.

Sangranita

Serves 8

Toby Keith made the red cups favored by frat boys famous, but I prefer an orange cup, especially one made from a real orange! This frosty dessert is a combination of a classic Spanish sangria and a frozen Italian granita.

1 cup red wine

¼ cup brandy

½ cup sugar

8 large seedless oranges

1 cup strawberries, sliced, fresh or frozen

Juice of 1 lemon

1 (8-ounce) can crushed pineapple, including juice

✤ In a saucepan, combine the wine, brandy, and sugar. Stir over medium heat until the sugar is dissolved. Remove from the heat.

✤ Rinse the oranges. Cut off the top of each orange at the blossom end to create a cup. Using a grapefruit knife, remove the meat, working just along the inside of the orange skin. Pour any juice or fruit fragments remaining on the bottom into the blender. Set the fruit aside. Cut a thin slice off the bottom of each orange shell, just above the stem end, about the size of a half dollar, so the orange will stand up on its own. Place the empty orange skins in the freezer.

✤ Chop the fruit from the oranges and put it in the blender. Blend until liquefied. Add the strawberries, pineapple, and lemon juice. Blend again. Add the blended fruit mixture to the saucepan with the wine, brandy and sugar. Stir well.

✤ Transfer the mixture to a 9 × 13-inch pan. Make sure the mixture is at room temperature. Place it in the freezer. Every 30 minutes or so, use a fork to scrape around the edges of the pan, mixing and breaking up lumps and chunks.

✤ The sangranita is done when it is completely frozen, about 2 to 3 hours. Scrape, or rake, the sangranita with a fork. Fill the orange cups with it, creating a mound on top. Return the cups to the freezer until ready to serve.

POSTSCRIPT

There will be more sangranita than needed to fill the orange cups. It freezes well in a covered container, or you can make sangranita ice cubes for white-wine spritzers and to spice up lemonade.

A Wine by Any Other Name

Sauvignon Blanc has been around for hundreds of years, but what about Fumé Blanc? It's also been around hundreds of years and it is the exact same varietal as Sauvignon Blanc.

Robert Mondavi gave Fumé Blanc its name in 1966. He coined the name to distinguish his dry Sauvignon Blanc from the sweet Sauvignon Blancs of the time. "Fumé" is sexier than "dry," *n'est-ce pas*? Sauvignon Blanc may not have been a big seller at the time, but Fumé Blanc became one. Mondavi is credited with popularizing the wine variety throughout the United States.

Similarly, White Zinfandel was given its name to make rosé wines, already long in existence, more appealing to American wine drinkers. Sutter Home Winery created the brand of White Zinfandel in the early 1970s. It is made from red Zinfandel grapes, and it is important to note there is no such thing as white Zinfandel grapes. Since most grape juice is actually water white, regardless of whether it is a white or a red grape, White Zinfandel gets it pink color from brief contact with the skin of the red grapes.

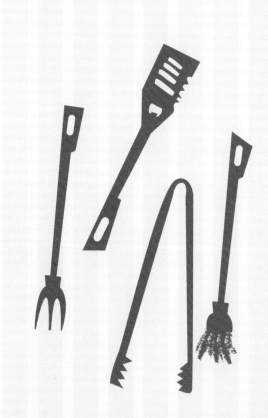

Aisle Eleven
housewares

Mother Told You Never to Play with Sharp Knives. She Was Wrong!

The sharper the knife, the more efficient the knife, the safer the knife. It's the dull ones that are dangerous!

Good knives are an investment. Treat yourself to professional sharpening at least once a year.

The attentive care doesn't end there. When you are done using knives, never put them in the dishwasher. The dishwasher is too rough for such a delicate utensil. It's also a no-no to let them sit in the sink. Wash and dry them immediately.

Always place your knives back in the block, dull side down, so there is no friction on the blade. If you don't have a block, do not put them loosely in a drawer. Buy a knife holder that is flat and fits inside your drawer or magnetic strip at your local culinary store.

Some Like It Hot

Liquids like soup can be deceptive when heated in the microwave. Water absorbs microwave energy especially fast, and it can heat to beyond boiling very quickly. It may look still in the container, but be careful, because if it's overheated, it may not start churning and bubbling until you move it.

Can't be latte for work? Then make steamed milk for your coffee in the microwave. Harold McGee, in his Curious Cook column, suggests putting cold milk in a sealed jar and shaking it until foamy. Remove the lid and heat in the microwave until hot.

Why Should You Listen to Your Knives?

Not sure if it's time to sharpen your knife? Listen to it. Carefully ping the blade. If you hear a high-pitched tone, the blade is still sharp. If you hear a dull tone, it's time to sharpen the knife.

Isinglass Is Not a Goblet for Your Chardonnay!

Ice in glass is recommended for enjoying ice-cold lemonade. Wordplay aside, isinglass is actually used for wine, although has nothing to do with glass or stemware. Made of dried sturgeon bladder, isinglass (pronounced "eyes-in-glass") is a substance wine-maker's use to polish and clarify white wine. The use of isinglass is a remedial process, assisting wines that are cloudy, and is not common in everyday winemaking.

Who knew that fish guts made clear wine?

Don't Do the Hokey-Pokey with Your Potato

According to the U.S. Potato Board, you don't need to poke holes in your potato when microwaving it. And if you don't, it will cook faster.

That's because approximately 80 percent of a fresh potato is water, and the microwave uses that water to create steam inside the skin. When you puncture the potato, the steam escapes, slowing down the cooking process.

Plus, it's really fun to prove to your pals it won't explode.

That said, the preferred method of cooking potatoes in the microwave is not poking holes with a fork (that's for potatoes baked in the oven). Instead, cut a thin wedge lengthwise in the potato, about ⅛ inch wide and 1 inch deep. Microwave uncovered, in a microwave-safe dish, on high for 10 to 12 minutes, and you'll end up with a spud with dry and fluffy pulp.

Zapped Potato Salad

Serves 8

Baking potatoes can take up to an hour. So why not zap them and get the picnic started sooner? This salad is dressed with the same toppings you'd use on a traditional baked potato, even though the potatoes are not baked. (That can be our little secret.)

4 large red potatoes, about 2 pounds

4 slices cooked bacon, chopped into small pieces

2 tablespoons chives, minced

1 cup sour cream

½ teaspoon garlic powder

½ teaspoon celery salt

½ cup white cheddar cheese, shredded

Salt and pepper to taste

✤ Wash and dry the potatoes. Cut a wedge in each one lengthwise, ⅛ inch wide and 1 inch deep. Microwave the potatoes in a microwave-safe dish until cooked, about 10 to 12 minutes. Remove the potatoes with oven mitts. Cool for 5 minutes, and then slice the potatoes in half, sliding your knife down the wedge lengthwise. Continue to cool until the potatoes reach room temperature.

✤ Cube the potatoes, leaving the skin on, and place the cubes in a large bowl. Mix in the bacon and chives. In a separate bowl, blend the sour cream, garlic powder, and celery salt. Pour it over the potatoes and toss. Gently mix in the white cheddar cheese. Season with salt and pepper to taste.

✤ It takes more time to cool the potatoes than to cook them in this recipe. However, if you're still tight for time, go ahead and substitute bacon bits and pre-shredded cheddar.

Stick It Out

It was difficult for me to embrace the heavy-gauge stainless-steel cookware I received as a wedding present. I had always used nonstick pots and pans. Sticky food left on stainless steel required scrubbing. Why go to all that work?

When I noticed that a chef pal didn't have any nonstick pans in his kitchen, he explained that it wasn't because he had a guy washing dishes in the back; it was because metals are the best conductors of heat.

Then he set me straight for cooking at home. It wasn't the pan's fault for the sticky mess—it was mine. Putting cold food into a cold pan was my mistake, and patience was the cure.

Always heat the pan on low to medium a few minutes before adding any oil or butter. Before adding food, the fats should be gently rippling. Hold your hand an inch above the pan to be sure there is enough heat to start cooking on contact. (Too much heat can cause your food to stick too.)

More patience is required when it comes to turning. Proteins will stick if you turn them too soon. Wait until the food has released and you can jiggle it easily in the pan before flipping it. If it requires pulling or tugging, it needs more time on that side.

Now I use my stainless-steel pots and pans every day. My food tastes better, and I threw away my scouring pads years ago.

Wax Poetic

I'm a romantic and use candles on the dinner table nearly every night. They are pretty when lit, but a mess when they burn out. I've been frustrated trying various methods to clean out the pooled wax. Residue was always left on the sides of the votives when I exacted the wax with a knife or put them in the dishwasher.

Then I discovered that heat wasn't as effective as cold for wax removal. Place the holders in the freezer after they cool. When frozen, the wax will solidify and pop out easily.

I haven't had a meltdown since.

What Can Baryshnikov Teach You About Sautéing?

"Sauté" comes from the French word *sauter*—"to jump."

You may not have seen Baryshnikov do a grand jeté, but I bet you've seen chefs make their minced onions "jump" by flipping the pan so they move from the back of the pan to the front. Proper sauté technique means you are cooking small amounts, usually in butter or oil, and moving them quickly.

It can be messy to learn to sauté like a chef on the stove. I suggest practicing with raw rice outside or over a sink. At first you may fling most of the rice outside of the pan, but with persistent practice, you'll be a pro at making your onions "jump."

Pizza Para-Box

You've finished your large pepperoni. The box is cardboard, so you put it in the recycling bin, and you feel pretty good about yourself for making the effort.

Me too. Except I have learned that it's a mistake. I was cleaning up at school after a party, thinking I was being a friend of the environment by carting eight empty pizza boxes to the recycling bin, when another mother scolded me. She asked if I had ever taken the time to read the directions on the recycling bin at home. I admitted that I had not, and that's when she set me straight.

Grease and cheese from pizza that is left on the box are contaminants; they taint legitimate recyclables. Those boxes must go in the garbage or compost.

Pizza boxes and all other paper products are only recyclable if they are free of food and oil. You can still help our environment by cutting off the offending areas of the pizza box and then recycling the clean cardboard.

The paradox? Jars, cans, and bottles with food in them are recyclable, because they can be washed.

How Your Wet/Dry Vac Can Make You a Better Cook

They don't call it a dry/wet vac, and that's good news to help you remember to always add your *wet* ingredients into your *dry* ingredients when mixing a batter. That will avoid lumps.

If you add your dry ingredients to wet, the tendency will be for the batter to clump, and you'll have to overmix to compensate, making it tough.

Grilled Pizzadillas

Serves 4

Homemade pizza dough is delicious but time-consuming to make. Ready-to-eat pizza dough is always an option; however, if you prefer thin crusts like me, it takes some skill to roll or toss them to the desired thickness. Flour tortillas to the rescue! They are tasty, convenient, and easy to use. Cooking them on the grill makes them smoky and crispy.

THE ITALIAN *PIZZA* VERSION

1 teaspoon olive oil

1 cup sliced mushrooms (you can use them raw if sliced thinly, but I precook mine)

4 (8-inch) multigrain flour tortillas (this size is much easier to handle than 10- or 12-inch tortillas)

4 paper plates (they make schlepping pizzadillas to and from the grill a lot easier)

¼ cup prepared pizza sauce

2 cups shredded pizza blend cheese

¾ cup sliced pepperoni

Pizza stone for grill (you can put pizzadillas directly on the grates; however, I prefer the stone)

✤ Heat the grill to high. If you are using a stone (and I hope you are), be sure and put it on the grates just after you start it, not after the grill is hot.

✤ Heat a pan on high. Add olive oil after it is hot. Cook the mushrooms at high heat so they brown and caramelize. Remove from heat. (See "What Can Rice Krispies Teach You About Cooking Mushrooms?," page 18.)

✤ Put one tortilla on each paper plate. Spread the pizza sauce on the tortillas. Scatter the cheese on top of the pizza sauce. Evenly distribute the pepperoni, then the mushrooms, on all four pizzadillas.

✤ Carry the pizzadillas to the grill, then slide them off the paper plates and on to the grates or stone.

✤ Grill the pizzadillas covered for 3 to 4 minutes, or until the cheese is melted and the tortilla edges are brown and crispy.

✤ Remove from the grill. Use a pizza cutter or sharp knife to cut each into four pieces.

THE MEXICAN *DILLA* VERSION

4 (8-inch) multigrain flour tortillas

4 paper plates

¼ cup refried beans (if canned, microwave briefly to make them soft)

4 tablespoons salsa

2 cups shredded Mexican blend cheese

1 cup shredded lettuce

1 cup finely chopped tomatoes

¼ cup finely minced white onion or green scallion

Sour cream

✤ Put one tortilla on each paper plate. Spread a thin layer of refried beans on each tortilla. Smear 1 tablespoon of salsa over the beans. Scatter the cheese on top.

✤ Carry the pizzadillas to the grill, then slide them off the paper plates and on to the grates or stone.

✤ Grill the pizzadillas covered for 3 to 4 minutes, or until the cheese is melted and the tortilla edges are brown and crispy.

✤ Remove from the grill. Top with lettuce, tomatoes, and onion.

✤ Use a pizza cutter or sharp knife to cut each into four pieces. Serve with a dollop of sour cream.

POSTSCRIPT

Pizzadillas make sumptuous starters. The variations are endless with the variety of tortilla flavors, spreads, and cheese. Don't use more than three toppings (not including sauce and cheese). Otherwise your pizzadilla will be too heavy to pick up and eat with your hands.

Ese-y to Eat

There is a noticeable difference between ChinESE and JapanESE chopsticks. Chinese chopsticks are rectangular, blunt, and usually 10 inches long. Japanese chopsticks are shorter, thinner, and tapered at the end.

I can't teach you how to use chopsticks, but I can tell you how to make learning easier. Place a small piece of paper, folded into a half-inch rectangle, in between the chopsticks at the base and secure with a rubber band. Fear not—that's not cheating. It's more like training wheels.

Clearing Up the Confusion

It makes sense that knives are set on the right side of our plate; most people are right-handed and hold their knife in their right hand. Glasses are also placed to the right of our plate. Beverages are poured from that side.

But left and right can be confusing when it comes to service in a restaurant. Which way do you lean when the food is coming and going?

The simple answer is that servers deliver food from the left and clear from the right. I've had trouble retaining this tidbit for years, until I created a mnemonic image. "Clear" and "right" both have five letters. Clear ends with an *r* and right begins with one: CLEARRIGHT.

By the process of elimination, you don't have to remember the serving side, but you still may have to lean when your meal arrives.

Saucepan Versus Sauce Pot

The primary difference is the handles. A saucepan is round, has straight or flared sides and has a *single* handle. A sauce pot is taller than it is wide and has straight sides and *two* loop handles.

But wait there's more. Another difference is the spelling. "Saucepan" is always one word. However, "sauce pot" can be one word or two. It's not that the name for any cooking vessel ending in "pan" is one word, because "fry pan" is two words and "stockpot" is one.

I checked my trusty resource books and there was no consensus. I took a field trip to several culinary stores and looked at online catalogs, and there wasn't any consistency there either. My Microsoft Word doesn't care if it is one word or two.

With more investigation I found that "sauce pot," one word or two, is a fairly esoteric term. "Large pot" or "6-quart pot" is used more often in recipes to describe the same thing.

No matter how it is spelled, consider using a sauce pot on a crowded stove, as its small handles will make room for long-handled saucepans and fry pans.

Why Do Chefs Wear Tuxedos in the Kitchen?

Chef coats look professional, and they are functional too.

They are classically white to denote cleanliness. They're double-breasted so that the sides can easily be reversed to hide stains. The extra layer of thickness insulates the wearer from the heat of the stove. The buttons are covered in cotton, because plastic might melt if the button came in contact with a hot pan. The sleeves are long to keep arms protected from burns.

But why the triangular shaped neckerchief? Practically speaking, the neckerchief, also known as a cravat, helps to absorb sweat. However, formally the neckerchief is known as a tie. It was created to formalize and complement the chef's uniform, much like a bow tie completes a tuxedo.

Hors d'Oeuvre Versus Appetizers

I've been using the terms "hors d'oeuvre" and "appetizers" interchangeably for years. However, they are as different as a canapé and an amuse bouche.

To begin with, that wasn't a typo in the title. "Hors d'oeuvre" is spelled without an *s*, regardless of how many pieces are passed. It means "outside of the work." We don't go to the works, and we don't eat hors d'oeuvres. With common usage, "hors d'oeuvres" with an *s* is perfectly acceptable, but surely by this aisle you know that I am finicky with words.

Hors d'oeuvre are served while guests are mingling during the cocktail hour. They are passed or served buffet-style, often as finger food, and eaten in one or two bites.

A canapé is generally a passed hors d'oeuvre, similar to a mini open-faced sandwich, consisting of a piece of bread, cracker, or pastry with a spread, a topping, and a garnish.

An amuse bouche is presented at the table, a small gift from the kitchen meant to entice you for the rest of the meal.

Appetizers are the first course and meant to whet the appetite. They are also referred to as starters, since they begin the meal. Appetizer portions are larger than hors d'oeuvre and usually eaten on a plate while the guests are seated at the table.

Open Cease-A-Me

If you've been confounded by why it's taking the roast so long to cook or the cake so long to bake, you may ask yourself how often you opened the door to check internal temperature, insert a toothpick, baste, or just gawk.

Every time you open the oven door, you lose fifty to one hundred degrees of heat. Start doing the math. You'll save energy. Your roast will cook more quickly. And your cake will bake in a shake.

Why Should You Poke a Hole in Your Raft?

Ever noticed the floating mass that rises to the top when you are making a consommé (perfectly clear broth)?

It's called a raft, and while it may be unsightly, it is important. The raft is formed as the ingredients rise to the surface, cook, and coagulate. You do not want to skim it off, and you don't want to stir it in either.

The raft is helping clarify your soup by trapping impurities brought up from the bottom of the pot as it simmers.

Don't let your raft get dry! Poke a hole in it with a small ladle to baste it.

When the flavors have fully developed, strain the consommé, taking care not to deflate, er, destroy the raft. If you do, some of the impurities will go back into your broth.

Chicken Corn-Ucopias

35 to 40 pieces

The discussion about whether "cornucopia" is one word or two helped launch *The Food Guy and Marcy Show*. Cornucopias are more than a Thanksgiving centerpiece. They're also an hors d'oeuvre that's rolled into a cone shape. Serve these with salsa and a dictionary.

2 tablespoons butter

¼ cup onion, minced

¼ cup red bell pepper, minced

1 ear of corn, kernels removed

1 cup rotisserie chicken, finely shredded

½ teaspoon salt

½ teaspoon chili powder

1 tablespoon cilantro, chopped

¾ cup jack cheese, shredded

10 to 12 king-size corn tortillas

✤ Preheat the oven to 350°F.

✤ Melt the butter in large skillet on low. Add the onion, red bell pepper, and corn kernels. Cook 3 to 4 minutes. Remove from the heat and place in large mixing bowl. Add the chicken, salt, chili powder, and cilantro. Mix well. Add in ½ cup jack cheese, reserving ¼ cup for finishing touches.

✤ Using a 3-inch cookie cutter, cut four circles from each of the 10 tortillas. If you can only get three per tortilla, that's fine. Use the extra 2 tortillas to get 36 pieces.

✤ To fill the corn-ucopias, put a large pinch of chicken mixture on the top of each tortilla circle and roll it into a cone shape. Give the mixture a push to keep it in the lower part of the cone and add more mixture if there is room. Sprinkle a little jack cheese on the exposed part of the corn-ucopia and secure with a toothpick. Place the corn-ucopias on a lightly greased or parchment-lined sheet pan. Bake 20 minutes.

✤ Serve on a warm platter with a small empty bowl to collect the used toothpicks.

Why Should We Sweat the Small Stuff?

Recipes often instruct you to "sweat" the onions. Does that mean cook them until they start to perspire?

That's a good visual. However, "sweat" means to sauté without color. Small pieces of vegetables are cooked (sometimes covered) in a small amount of fat over low heat until they are soft, but not brown.

What Can a Wurlitzer Tell You About Your Taste Buds?

They are both organs.

You're probably familiar with the instrument that accompanies hymns at church, but you may not be familiar with the term for the perception of your sensory organs—including taste and aroma—when tasting your food: organoleptic.

It's organoleptic anytime you are involving your sense organs, including when you hear the sound of food, like the crispy crunch of fried chicken, or see food, such as the unsettling sight of brown guacamole.

I have loved this word ever since the first time I heard it, and I had to pipe in and pass it along to you.

Real or Imitation?

Orville Redenbacher was a real person, and Captain Crunch is a fictional cereal character. Easy, huh? What about Chef Boyardee, Aunt Jemima, Mrs. Paul, Dr Pepper, and Mrs. Cubbison?

Hector Boiardi emigrated from Italy when he was a teenager. He was the chef at the Plaza Hotel in New York by the time he was seventeen, and at nineteen catered President Woodrow Wilson's wedding. When he started his ravioli company with his brothers, he changed the spelling of Boiardi to Boyardee, so it would look like it sounded.

Sophie Cubbison cooked for laborers on her family's lima-bean farm from the age of sixteen; she saved enough money cooking five meals a day to put herself through college and earn a home economics degree. Mrs. Cubbison did not invent stuffing, but her brand and original recipes popularized the dish in America.

Aunt Jemima was the name of a ready-made pancake mix developed in 1889 by the Pearl Milling Company. Aunt Jemima the character came to life a year later when Nancy Green was hired to be the spokeswoman. Over time, other actresses have played the role of the beloved fictional cook.

Mrs. Paul is the mother of John Paul, cofounder of the frozen seafood business. Paul's partner was Edward Piszek. His mother lobbied to be the company's namesake, but apparently Mrs. Piszek's Fish Sticks didn't sound as appealing as Mrs. Paul's.

Dr Pepper is not a real person, although the soda was invented in a drugstore by a real person. Pharmacist Charles Alderton liked to mix carbonated beverages as much as he did medications. When he perfected the recipe for his soda in 1885, the drugstore's owner, Wade Morrison, named it Dr Pepper, allegedly for the father of a long-lost love. Dr Pepper is America's oldest major soft drink company. —P.S. The period after "Dr" was dropped in the 1950s.

Should You Ask Karen?

If you want to know if it's time to toss the canned goods, whether it's safe to thaw meat in hot water, or the merits of plastic versus wooden cutting boards, Karen can tell you. The virtual expert answers food safety concerns twenty-four hours a day, seven days a week.

You can contact Karen on the USDA website, askkaren.gov (she speaks English and Spanish). You can also reach her via a mobile app—just enter "m.askkarren.gov" in the browser of your smart phone.

Live online chat with a food-safety expert is available Monday through Friday, 10:00 A.M. to 4:00 P.M. EST year-round by dialing 1-888-674-6854.

How Can the Letters B and D Help You Set the Table?

If you take both hands, make "okay" signs, then press your pinky, ring, and middle fingers tightly together and straight upright, you will make a lower case *b* in your left hand and a lower case *d* in your right hand.

Now what?

Let the *b* on your left hand guide you to place the bread plate on the left. The *d* on the right hand tells you to put the drinks on the right.

It's a great tool to teach kids how to set the table, and if you're in a fancy restaurant and don't know where to put your dinner roll, go back to *b*.

Do You Have a Good Rack?

Well, you should. Both men and women. Every good cook needs one.

Not the rack that you dry your dishes in or any other rack your mind just conjured up—a rack for cooking meat in the oven.

Always elevate your meat. That way the heat can move around it evenly. If you put the meat directly on the bottom of the pan, the bottom won't brown and the weight will draw out the juices.

It doesn't have to be one of those fancy pans with a built-in rack. A flat rack like the ones used to cool cookies works fine when set in a sheet pan. Or build a veggie rack with celery stalks, whole carrots, and potatoes.

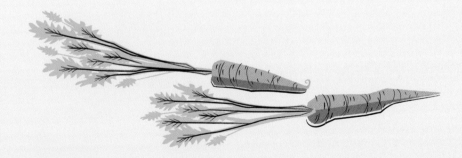

Bean There, Done That!

You need a big jolt of caffeine, so you ask your barista for the dark roast, right? Wrong. I was doing it myself for years, but now I know that darker coffee beans have slightly less caffeine than lighter roasts. It's a small distinction, but a fun one.

Next, although it is a fast, or express, drink to make, there is no *x* in "espresso." Second and more important, espresso has less caffeine than drip coffee! That's because the water is passing through the coffee very quickly, 20 to 30 seconds, much faster than the brewing method where it steeps a while.

Decaffeinated coffee is not caffeine-free. Decaffeination is a process where almost all, but not 100 percent, of the caffeine, is removed. Brewed coffee averages 95 to 200 milligrams caffeine per 8 ounces; decaffeinated coffee has between 2 and 12 milligrams for the same size serving.

Sweet or Sweetened?

The major difference between sweet tea and sweetened iced tea is not just the South; it's the sugar and, more specifically, when it was added.

Sweet tea is made by adding sugar while the tea is still hot. Iced tea is brewed black, then chilled, with the sweeteners added after it is served.

Sweet or sweetened, cold iced tea is far and away the most popular way to enjoy tea in America. Approximately 80 percent of us prefer our tea iced and cold rather than hot.

Sanka Very Much

Here's the scoop. Decaffeinated coffee was invented in Germany by Ludwig Roselius around 1906. Legend has been brewing that it was named Sanka for the French word *sans,* meaning "without" (caffeine), and *Ka,* the beginning of the German word *Kaffee,* "coffee."

General Foods acquired the brand for the United States. Later, Maxwell House created the bright orange label to separate their instant Sanka decaf from the rest of the caffeinated coffee brands on the shelf.

The color orange and Sanka became iconic for identifying decaffeinated coffee. Diners and coffee shops still use orange-rimmed pots with orange handles for decaf today.

Orange Pekoe-Boo

Tea time just got more interesting. Here are two tea fun facts.

Orange pekoe tea often comes in an orange container, but it is not orange flavored. The name refers to the grade of the tea leaf, which is measured by size.

Although it is acceptable to pronounce it "*peek*-oh," as in *peek*-a-boo, the Chinese pronounce it "*peck*-oh."

Orange you glad to know this?

Riley Rose's Ribs

Serves 4 to 6 as a main course or 10 as an hors d'oeuvre

I won't call my daughter, Riley Rose, a picky eater. I prefer the term *selective*. But she loves ribs! When you're making your tea in the morning, make a few extra cups for the marinade (even faster, use 2 cups premade sweet tea and omit molasses).

4 pounds baby back ribs (ideally two racks at 2 pounds each)

FOR THE MARINADE

3 orange pekoe tea bags (Lipton's Yellow Label Tea is a blend of orange and black pekoe tea)

2 cups water

½ cup apple cider vinegar

¼ cup soy sauce

½ cup molasses

¼ cup Dijon mustard

½ cup olive oil

3 garlic cloves

3 sprigs rosemary

FOR THE GLAZE

½ cup orange marmalade

¼ cup soy sauce

1 tablespoon white wine vinegar

Pinch of red pepper flakes

✢ Preheat the oven to 300°F.

✢ Cut the racks in half, but no smaller, as presliced ribs will dry out quickly while cooking.

✢ Boil the water and brew the tea. Be sure your final yield is a full 2 cups.

✢ In a medium-size bowl add the vinegar, soy sauce, molasses, and mustard. Slowly whisk in the olive oil.

✢ Add the tea to the mixture, whisk all the ingredients one more time, and place the mixture in the refrigerator to cool, about 30 minutes.

✢ Transfer the mixture to a 1-gallon resealable plastic bag. Add the whole garlic cloves, rosemary, and ribs. Squeeze out all the air and seal the bag

tightly. Give it a few shakes to immerse the ribs in the marinade and put it in the refrigerator. Marinate for 8 hours, turning the bag several times.

✢ To make the glaze, put all the ingredients in a small sauce pot. Heat over medium-low until marmalade is dissolved. Turn off the heat and set the pan aside.

✢ Remove the ribs from the refrigerator. Discard the marinade. Let the ribs stand for 20 minutes. Put the ribs on a rack on top of a sheet pan lined with foil.

✢ Bake 1½ to 2 hours or until the meat begins to pull from the bones. Add the glaze during the final 10 minutes of cooking.

✢ Allow the ribs to rest 10 minutes, then serve.

You Wouldn't Wear White After Labor Day, Would You? Then Don't Drink Cappuccino After 11:00 A.M.

My first rule about food is that there are no rules.

That said, Italians love their traditions, and they consider cappuccino a morning beverage and occasionally a stand-alone snack.

The tradition comes with a reason, and the reason is digestion. Breakfast is light in Italy—typically bread or a sweet roll with a cappuccino or espresso. Lunch and dinner, however, tend to be heavier. Finishing the bigger meals with cappuccino and all that milk slows digestion.

Therefore you'll rarely, if ever, see Italians drinking a cappuccino after 11:00 A.M. They tend to consider tourists who indulge in the frothy coffee after a meal in the afternoon or evening heathens.

The no-rules rule?

Others may have looked askance, but I have worn white pumps in October and I've had cappuccino after lasagna.

Afternoon Tea Versus High Tea

The only thing that afternoon tea and high tea have in common is that they are both British traditions. Is high tea more elegant than afternoon tea?

Not exactly. Afternoon tea is a light repast with tea, a few sweets, and small sandwiches. High tea is served in the late afternoon or early evening. Crumpets and clotted cream are included, however; it's considerably more of a meal than afternoon tea, featuring meat, fish, and other entrees.

Coffee Connoisseur?

It's only the best when it comes to your coffee. How many of these things have you done to ensure you have the best cup possible?

1. Use a high-quality coffee maker or French Press.

2. Keep the coffee-making equipment clean at all times.

3. If your tap water is not tasty, use filtered or bottled water.

4. Always start with cold water.

5. Buy fresh whole coffee beans.

6. Own a mill and grind the beans only right before brewing.

7. Use a ratio of 6 ounces of water for every 1 to 2 tablespoons of ground coffee.

8. Store coffee beans you are not using in the freezer.

Did you answer yes to all eight questions? If you did, your coffee probably tastes good, but it has probably not realized its full potential.

According to the National Coffee Association, storing your coffee in the freezer or refrigerator is not ideal, as the moisture will cause the coffee to deteriorate. It recommends keeping coffee away from excessive air, moisture, heat, and light.

The last line on the quiz should have read:

8. Store coffee beans in an airtight container in a dark and cool location.

Bubbie's BBQ Sauce

2 cups

I first met Maxine Bloom, whom I affectionately call Bubbie in the Jewish tradition, at the meat counter of our local supermarket. Our conversation was instantly lively, and much to the chagrin of our fellow shoppers, we were oblivious to the fact that our carts were blocking the aisle. When Bubbie told me she was a recipe tester for Carol Field and Cindy Pawlcyn, I was surprised to learn that chefs used professional recipe testers. Intrigued, I invited her to be a guest on *The Food Guy and Marcy Show* and, later, to test recipes for this book. Bubbie is an old-world, from-scratch cook. She never, ever, buys bottled anything. Her BBQ sauce is worthy of the brief time it takes to make.

1 onion, finely chopped

1 clove garlic, or more to taste, chopped

2 cups tomato puree

½ cup black coffee

½ teaspoon thyme

½ teaspoon nutmeg

2 tablespoons molasses

3 tablespoons vinegar

3 tablespoons brown sugar

2 tablespoons Dijon mustard

1 teaspoon salt

1 teaspoon pepper

Red pepper to taste

✤ Simmer all the ingredients for 20 minutes.

Creativi-Tea

The next time you use a tea bag, don't thank Mr. Lipton. Thank Mr. Sullivan.

Thomas Sullivan was an enterprising tea merchant in New York at the turn of the century. Looking to minimize his expenses shipping tea to potential retailers, he packed his tea in small quantities in a silk bag.

It was a good idea, as shipping tea in tin cans was far more costly. However, he didn't include instructions. When the recipients received Mr. Sullivan's samples, they did not take the tea out of the bags before brewing. They thought the bag was an alternative to a tea infuser.

Mr. Sullivan's tea-riffic, albeit accidental, idea was rewarded with a deluge of orders for his individually packed and disposable tea bags.

College Athletes and Coffee

Athletes are always looking for the extra edge, but can the edge given to you by caffeine enhance performance?

Apparently so, because the NCAA lists caffeine among the "Drugs and Procedures Subject to Restriction." When student athletes are tested, they may be in violation if "caffeine concentrations in urine exceed 15 micrograms per milliliter." That would allow for several cups of coffee or cans of cola, but not much more.

It's Not Tea for Two—It's Tea for One

Black tea, oolong tea, green tea, and even white tea have one thing in common—besides being tea, of course. Despite being distinctly different teas, they all come from the same tea bush, *Camellia sinensis.* Yup, one bush, although there are hundreds of varietals.

(Herbal teas, including chamomile and mint, are the exception. Their flavor comes from a combination of herbs, spices, and botanicals and are more accurately called a *tisane.*)

The flavor, aroma, and color of tea are determined by how the camellia leaves are harvested, the way in which they are processed, and the extent of fermentation (if any).

Eighty percent of tea consumed in the world is black tea, which is fermented, as opposed to oolong tea, which is only partially fermented. Jasmine tea is a green or black tea that has been scented with the fragrant jasmine flower.

Then there is the tea-ography. Ceylon is tea grown in Sri Lanka. Darjeeling, known as the "champagne of teas," is a superior-quality black tea grown in the Himalayan Mountains of northern India. Formosa tea comes from Taiwan.

The next time you enjoy tea, marvel at the vast assortment of choices and the fact that they all come from the same bush the Chinese discovered over five thousand years ago.

Et-Tea-Quette

When you order tea in a restaurant, you are presented with a mini pot of hot water and one tea bag.

But what if you want more? Order a second cup, with fresh water and a fresh tea bag. One tea bag is not meant to brew several cups of tea.

This may seem like a rather steep request. However, tea aficionados insist on a new tea bag for each new cup of tea.

Raspberry Lemonade Mar-Tea-Ni

Arnold Palmer made the beverage of half lemonade and half iced tea famous. In this recipe, raspberry tea ice cubes slowly melt in the lemonade. Raspberry vodka gives the cocktail a blast of fruit and fun.

Serves 4

2 raspberry tea bags

1 cup boiling water

Ice-cube tray that makes 16 cubes (found in housewares or frozen-foods section)

4 martini glasses, chilled in freezer

2 cups prepared lemonade

4 jiggers raspberry vodka (12 tablespoons)

Cocktail shaker

FOR THE RASPBERRY ICE-TEA CUBES

✤ Add the tea bags to the boiling water. Steep until concentrated, about 30 minutes.

✤ Pour the tea into the ice-cube tray and freeze. (It should take 30 to 60 minutes, depending on how cold your freezer is.)

FOR THE COCKTAIL

✤ Remove the martini glasses and raspberry ice-tea cubes from the freezer. Place four raspberry tea ice cubes in each martini glass.

✤ Put the lemonade and raspberry vodka in the shaker and mix well.

✤ Pour evenly into the martini glasses, and serve immediately.

POSTSCRIPT:

For a nonalcoholic version, use a tall glass. Put eight raspberry tea ice cubes in each glass and fill with the lemonade.

Aisle Thirteen

chips, crackers, cookies, candy

What Do Secretariat and Potato Chips Have in Common?

Saratoga. The town in upstate New York is also the name for one of the world's most famous racetracks. Secretariat lost to Onion there—perfect for a food book, I know—in 1973, just after he won the Triple Crown.

Saratoga Springs is the birthplace of the potato chip. Legend has it that in the mid-nineteenth century, at Moon's Lake House Restaurant, a customer sent back his fried potatoes to the chef, grumbling that they were too soggy and too thick.

Furious with the returned food, yet determined to make the customer happy, the chef fried thinly sliced potatoes in hot oil, salted them, and presented them to the picky eater, who apparently approved.

The new-fangled potatoes were added to the menu and named "Saratoga Chips." From there the phenomenon evolved into the snack food we all know and love today.

Potato Chips and BBQ Dip

I admit that most of my chips come from a bag with "Ruffles" on the label, but it really is worth the effort to make potato chips at home. They'll fly off your counter faster than chocolate chip cookies fresh from the oven. Don't say I didn't warn you. Serve them with the BBQ Dip (the twist here is that instead of the flavor being in the chip, it's in the dip).

CHIPS

Make as many as you want, but you probably should make extra

Peanut oil for frying

Potatoes, preferably Russet (one large potato makes about 35 chips)

Sea salt

✤ Peel the potatoes. Slice them thinly, ideally with a food processor or mandolin, but a sharp knife will work. Lay the potato slices on a paper towel and pat them dry.

✤ In a large, heavy skillet, put enough oil to cover the pan ½ inch deep. Make sure that the oil is hot enough by dropping an end scrap of potato in it. If it sizzles on contact, the oil is ready.

✤ Add the potatoes in batches. Turn them occasionally. Be careful not to crowd the pan. Fry until nicely browned and crisp, about 5 minutes.

✤ Drain on clean paper towels and season with salt. Serve chips ASAP.

BBQ DIP

2 cups

2 cups sour cream

1 envelope Lipton's Onion Soup and Dip Mix

2 tablespoons chili powder

2 teaspoons garlic powder

1 teaspoon curry powder

✤ Mix all the ingredients together and serve with warm chips.

What Cookie Has Been to the Moon and Back Five Times?

Ever since the Oreo cookie was invented over one hundred years ago, Nabisco has baked enough cookies to reach the moon and back five times. That's more trips than Neil Armstrong made as an astronaut. If all the Oreos ever made were lined up side by side, they would circle the earth more than 380 times.

Another number features prominently with Oreo cookies—twelve. I counted and there are twelve flowers, dashes, and dots on each side.

There is a street called Oreo Way in New York City. It's off Ninth Avenue between Fifteenth and Sixteenth Streets; it's Oreo's birthplace and the site of Nabisco's first factory.

Can Vegetarians Eat Gummy Bears?

I'm sure vegetarians wouldn't want to pig out on a grizzly, but they may not realize that the gelatin in the candy is made from animal skins, cartilage, and bones.

That doesn't necessarily mean that vegetarians can't enjoy the chewy treats. Check your labels carefully, because nongelatin and vegan varieties are available.

What Do a Candy Bar and a Horse Have in Common?

"Snicker" means to give a suppressed laugh. It's also the word for a horse's whinny and the name of the world's most popular candy bar.

The Mars Company named its chocolate bar packed with peanuts, caramel, and nougat for the Mars family's favorite horse, Snickers, in 1930.

Why Should You Bring Chocolate to the Beach?

It may seem counterintuitive to bring a candy that melts as easily as chocolate to the warm beach. However, German researchers have found that dark chocolate may act as a sunscreen and prevent skin damage.

Wilhelm Stahl of Heinrich-Heine University in Dusseldorf led a study with women ages eighteen to sixty-five. The subjects who drank a specially prepared cocoa packed with flavonoids (potent antioxidants) for three months had less skin reddening after being exposed to ultraviolet light than their counterparts. Their skin was also moister and less scaly.

These findings are only preliminary, continue to wear sunscreen, but it can't hurt to eat chocolate to boost your SPF a bit.

Why Are There Snowflakes and Mushrooms in Your Popcorn?

Popcorn comes in two basic shapes, snow-flake and mushroom. Movie theaters and ballparks use the snowflake variety, because it pops bigger. Candy confections are made with mushroom popcorn, because it doesn't crumble.

Popcorn is a pop-ular and healthy whole-grain snack too. Air-popped popcorn has 31 calories per cup and, surprisingly, oil-popped popcorn comes in at only 55 calories per cup.

If you're looking for popcorn that won't get stuck in your teeth or braces, try hull-less sorghum popcorn. Although it's a new snack in America, sorghum is an ancient grain that people in India and Africa have been eating for years. Sorghum popcorn is made from a cereal grain that can be popped just like regular popcorn. It's smaller than the movie-theater variety and has a nutty taste.

Mama Frischkorn's Caramel Corn

Recipe courtesy of Chef Eric Frischkorn and the Kendall-Jackson Wine Center

3 quarts

Guy and I recorded *The Food Guy and Marcy Show* at the Kendall-Jackson Wine Center. Thanks to Executive Chef Justin Wangler and his team, our guests were gifted with the center's signature caramel corn. I think it was one reason they returned again and again to join us on our show. As a dessert, it pairs beautifully with Kendall-Jackson's late harvest Chardonnay.

½ cup butter

¼ cup light corn syrup

1 cup brown sugar

2 teaspoons kosher salt

½ teaspoon vanilla

¼ teaspoon baking soda

3 quarts air-popped popcorn (preferred, but stovetop popcorn will also work)

✤ Preheat the oven to 300°F. Grease a foil-lined cookie sheet with nonstick spray.

✤ In a 1-gallon heavy-bottomed saucepan, melt the butter over medium heat. Add the corn syrup and brown sugar, stirring to combine. Simmer until large bubbles begin to form without agitating the pan, approximately 4 minutes. Continue cooking on medium heat and stir every 30 seconds for the next 4 to 6 minutes. (To check the color of the caramel at this point, carefully dip one piece of the popped corn into the pot. The caramel should be amber in color.)

✤ Turn off the heat and carefully whisk in the salt, vanilla, and baking soda. Fold in the popped corn and gently coat it without crushing it.

✤ Transfer the popcorn to the greased cookie sheet and bake at 300º F. Gently stir it every 5 minutes for 15 minutes, making sure all the popcorn is evenly coated.

✤ Remove and cool the finished caramel corn on wax paper. Once cool enough to handle, but not completely cold, break apart the popcorn bunches.

Why Uneeda Graham Cracker

Before there was the snack treat we enjoy in s'mores, there was Graham flour, named for its inventor—vegetarian and food reformer Dr. Sylvester Graham.

Graham, who was also a reverend, was a healthy-diet crusader in the 1830s. He preached a mostly raw, plant-based diet without meat, coffee, or alcohol. He advocated for whole grains, including his coarsely ground whole-wheat Graham flour, which was baked into brown "Graham Bread."

Mrs. Lincoln's Boston Cookbook published a Graham cracker recipe in 1884 that included sugar and butter. Dr. Graham didn't live to see this heretical use of his product. He died in 1851.

Several bakeries with their own Graham crackers followed. They joined together in 1898 to form the National Biscuit Company, which would later be shortened to Nabisco.

The Pacific Coast Biscuit Company introduced the Honey Maid version in 1925 (later acquired by Nabisco). It was called Uneeda Graham Cracker. The pun, good as it is, wasn't intentional. The name of the bakery was Uneeda Bakers.

When you're in New York City, a fun food field trip is visiting the former Nabisco factory that is now the Chelsea Market. Built in the 1890s, it's a mini museum with shops and restaurants. You might even see your favorite Food Network star sipping coffee or munching a sandwich—the Food Network studios are upstairs.

Happy Campers S'mores

Think outside the graham-cracker box! My pal Nancy Lasseter and I concocted these sweet and savory s'mores at a KOA campground in Cloverdale, California. For an indoor s'mores buffet, use s'mores makers, available at most big-box stores.

SWEET S'MORES:

Chocolate graham crackers, After Eight mints, marshmallows

✤ Roast a marshmallow. Place an After Eight mint on a graham cracker, and the roasted marshmallow on top of the After Eight mint. Top with another graham cracker.

Chocolate graham crackers, white chocolate bars, marshmallows

✤ Roast a marshmallow. Place white chocolate on a graham cracker, and the roasted marshmallow on top of the white chocolate. Top with another graham cracker.

Pepperidge Farm Bordeaux cookies; Kraft caramel candies, sliced in half, or caramel sauce; pears

✤ Roast half a seeded pear and slice it. Place a thin piece of caramel on a Bordeaux cookie, and a hot slice of pear on top of the caramel. Top with another Bordeaux cookie.

Pepperidge Farm Gingerman cookies; Kraft caramel candies, sliced in half, or caramel sauce; marshmallows

✤ Roast a marshmallow. Place a thin piece of caramel on a Gingerman cookie, and the roasted marshmallow on top of the caramel. Top with another Gingerman cookie.

Graham crackers, Reese's Peanut Butter Cups, chocolate graham crackers, marshmallows

✤ Roast a marshmallow. Place a Reese's Peanut Butter Cup on a graham cracker, and the roasted marshmallow on top of the peanut butter cup. Top with a chocolate graham cracker.

Cinnamon graham crackers, apple slices, marshmallows

✤ Roast a marshmallow. Place a thin apple slice on a cinnamon graham cracker, and the roasted marshmallow on top of the apple slice. Top with another cinnamon graham cracker.

Girl Scout Thin Mint cookies (the chocolate is built in!), marshmallows

✤ Roast a marshmallow. Place the marshmallow on a Girl Scout Thin Mint cookie and top with another Girl Scout Thin Mint cookie.

Graham crackers, Nutella, bananas

✤ Slice a banana crosswise in half. Roast it until hot and soft and cut it into round slices. Spread Nutella on a graham cracker, and place slices of banana on top of the Nutella. Top with another Graham cracker.

(continued)

SAVORY S'MORES:

Butter crackers, sliced tomatoes, a small mozzarella ball (sometimes called a bocconcino)

✤ Roast the mozzarella ball. Place a tomato slice on a butter cracker, and top with hot mozzarella. Top with another butter cracker.

Water crackers, goat cheese, figs

✤ Roast a fig with the skin on and then slice it. Place a slice of goat cheese on a water cracker, and top with a slice of fig. Top with another water cracker.

Cheese crackers, half-slices of cooked bacon, lettuce, halved Roma tomatoes

✤ Roast a tomato half. Place lettuce and a bacon half-slice on a cheese cracker, and top with the roasted tomato half. Top with another cheese cracker.

Pepper Crackers, Boursin or other spreadable cheese, asparagus spears

✤ Cut the asparagus in 2-inch pieces and place on a skewer.

Roast the asparagus. Spread cheese on a pepper cracker, and top with two or three roasted asparagus pieces. Top with another pepper cracker.

Mushroom caps, goat cheese (or other soft cheese)

✤ Stuff the mushroom cap with goat cheese. Place the skewer horizontally through center of the mushroom, and roast until the mushroom is soft and just leaking juices.

Round tortilla chips, refried beans, mild Anaheim chilis

✤ Roast a chili and cut into pieces. (The size depends on how spicy you like it.) Spread refried beans on a round tortilla chip, and top with roasted Anaheim chili pieces. Top with another round tortilla chip.

Cocktail rye bread, tuna salad, chunk of cheddar cheese

✤ Roast the cheddar cheese. Spread tuna salad on a piece of cocktail rye, and top with roasted cheese. Top with another slice of cocktail rye.

Equipment to Make You a Happier Camper

There are specially designed two-pronged forks that prevent marshmallows from slipping into the fire while roasting. As an alternate cooking method, wrap s'mores in foil and heat in the oven or fire pit. The "Happy Campers S'mores" demonstration video is on my YouTube channel, MarcyAdventures.

Should You Brush Your Teeth with Chocolate?

According to a study conducted at Tulane University, chocolate may be as good as, or perhaps even better, than fluoride for preventing cavities.

The secret is the cocoa extract. The cocoa extract helps harden tooth enamel. The harder the tooth enamel, the less likely teeth will decay.

Adding fluoride to toothpaste was a breakthrough in 1914. Imagine adding chocolate in the twenty-first century!

What Does a Street Name Have to Do with a Stacked Snack?

You probably already guessed that I'm talking about Pringles, the chips that are uniformly shaped and stacked in a can to prevent breakage.

What you may not know is how Procter & Gamble came upon the name Pringles. It was suggested by an employee who drove past Pringle Drive, a street in Cincinnati close to where the company headquarters are located. The company liked the alliteration of the P's: potato chip, Pringles, and Procter & Gamble.

Pringles are closer to a fried mashed potato than a fried potato chip. In order to be called a chip they must start with whole potatoes; Pringles are made with dried potatoes (equivalent to three or four potatoes per can) that have been cooked and mashed, then fried and seasoned on one side.

The Big Ten Takes a Licking

Football, basketball, and baseball. Those are all Big Ten pursuits, but what about licking?

Engineering students at Purdue University and the University of Michigan were intrigued by the question: How many licks does it take to get to the Tootsie Roll center of the Tootsie Pop? They both built licking machines to mimic the action of the human tongue in an effort to determine the number of licks needed.

The score?

Purdue 364, Michigan 411.

Since the goal is to make the Tootsie Pop last as long as possible, Michigan "won," since its device required more licks than Purdue's did.

It's All It's Cracked Up to Be

Sometime during the mid-eighteenth century, the English biscuit was renamed a cracker in America. It happened when a biscuit was broken into pieces and it made a cracking noise.

Crackers that are leavened with bicarbonate of soda, aka baking soda (or that yellow box in the back of your fridge), are known as soda crackers.

Matzo is an unleavened cracker.

Water crackers are typically made with flour, water, oil, and salt.

Those little ditties we use on top of seafood chowder? You know them as oyster crackers, but you can also call them "Trentons," named after the bakery that created them in Trenton, New Jersey.

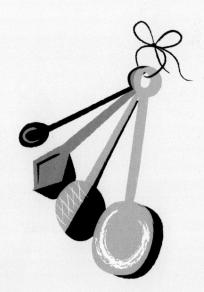

refrigerated foods

What Do Disneyland's Haunted Mansion and the Pillsbury Doughboy Have in Common?

When you enter the Haunted Mansion you hear, "Welcome, foolish mortals . . . I am your host—your Ghost Host." That is the voice of Paul Frees, who was also the voice of Poppin' Fresh, the Pillsbury Doughboy. Woo-hoo!

The Doughboy first appeared in a Pillsbury crescent roll commercial in 1965. The Ghost Host first greeted guests in Disneyland's Haunted Mansion in 1969. Paul Frees had a rare four-octave vocal range, which accounts for his deep timber as the Ghost Host and high-pitched squeal as the Pillsbury Doughboy.

Doughboy Breakfast Rolls

Pillsbury Crescent Rolls were a staple at holiday dinners when I was growing up in the San Fernando Valley. I take them to a new level, and a new time of day, with these kid-friendly, eat-with-your-hands breakfast rolls. Nothing says lovin' like somethin' from the oven.

Serves 8

8 slices pancetta or 8 strips bacon, chopped

1 tablespoon butter

½ small red bell pepper, diced

6 eggs

½ cup cheddar cheese, shredded

4 tablespoons chives, or more to taste, minced

1 (8-ounce) can Pillsbury Crescent Rolls

✤ Preheat the oven to 350°F.

✤ Cook the pancetta or bacon in a hot skillet until browned. Remove and drain on paper towels. Wipe the excess oil from the pan.

✤ Melt the butter in the pan and add the red bell peppers. Cook 5 minutes. Add the eggs and stir gently a few times. Add the cheese. Cook until the eggs are just beginning to set, but not completely cooked.

Remove the eggs from heat sooner than you normally would, as they will continue cooking in the oven. Mix in the chives and pancetta or bacon and set aside.

✤ Unfold the rolls and place them on an ungreased cookie sheet. Spoon 2 teaspoons of the egg mixture into the center of the dough and roll into a crescent shape. Bake for 13 to 15 minutes.

What Is a Flag Doing on Pizza?

The classic pizza margherita was created in Naples in 1889. It was made with mozzarella, tomato sauce, and basil—white, red, and green for the colors of the Italian flag.

The *tricolore* pie isn't symbolic just for its colors. It was named for the queen of Italy at the time, Margherita di Savoia (1851–1926).

Butter Basics

Sweet cream butter (by law) must be at least 80 percent fat. The other 20 percent is a mixture of mostly water.

Whipped butter is softened sweet butter that is injected with nitrogen gas—up to one-third of its volume. (Notably not air. Harold McGee explains in *On Food and Cooking* that air encourages rancidity.)

Salted sweet cream butter contains up to 2 percent salt. The salt is added primarily to extend shelf life, not for flavor.

Unsalted butter is generally favored by chefs and bakers, because they like to control the amount of salt that goes into their dishes. It also tends to be fresher and more perishable, because salt isn't added to preserve the butter.

Always wrap your butter or keep it in a covered dish, as it absorbs odors easily.

Bakin' Bacon

I love bacon on Sunday morning, although I hate the mess, not to mention the hassle of keeping it warm while my family sleeps.

I've fried it, used one of those plastic devices in the microwave, and prepared it on the griddle with a cast-iron bacon weight. After years of using all of those techniques I've hit upon the one that works for me—the oven.

I place parchment paper on a sheet pan and bake the bacon at 400°F for 15 to 20 minutes, depending on its size and thickness. Since the bacon self-bastes, no turning is required and clean up is as easy as throwing the greasy parchment paper away.

Then I use a pro's trick. Chef Les Goodman taught me at Charlie Palmer's *Dry Creek Kitchen* to put bread slices directly on the just-used sheet pan, place the crispy bacon on top of it, and then leave it in the oven at the lowest heat until it is ready to be served. The bread absorbs some of the grease, and the radiant heat from the sheet pan keeps the bacon warm without overcooking it.

The bakin' bacon bread is great toasted for a BLT, dried for croutons, or stale in a bread salad.

Bakin' Bacon Bread Salad

Serves 4 to 6

If there was ever an excuse to make bacon, this may be it! After you're done bakin' bacon in the morning, be sure to use the leftover bread and all its deliciousness for this classic Italian bread salad for dinner.

DRESSING

½ cup olive oil

1 clove garlic, minced

1 teaspoon Dijon mustard

2 tablespoons red wine vinegar

Salt and pepper to taste

✤ Whisk all the dressing ingredients in a glass or stainless steel bowl. You can also use the blender or put all the ingredients in a glass jar and shake well.

SALAD

8-ounces sourdough or ciabatta bread prepared as in "Bakin' Bacon," page 244, or regular day-old bread, cubed

2 cups cherry tomatoes, halved (ideally red and yellow or heirloom)

1 medium shallot, minced

1 English cucumber quartered lengthwise, cut in ½-inch pieces

8 slices cooked bacon (see "Bakin' Bacon," page 244), cut in ½-inch pieces

✤ Place all the salad ingredients in a large mixing bowl. Add the dressing and mix well with your hands. Let salad sit on the counter for 1 hour, so that the flavors meld and the tomatoes release their juices. Do not put the salad in the refrigerator.

Got Milk?

If you were given a female calf, how soon until you could milk her? Three months? Six months? A year?

It may seem udderly obvious, but first she has to go from being a heifer, a cow that has not had a calf of her own, to a mommy—that usually happens at around two years old. The only way a cow makes milk is just like a human—after she has given birth.

A cow lactates for about three hundred days. After that, in order to continue producing milk, she will need to get pregnant again.

The average dairy cow works five to six years and gives 6 gallons of milk per day.

Solid Advice

A solid fat is any type of fat that becomes solid at room temperature. These fats tend to come from dairy and meat animals. They include milk fat, butter, shortening, stick margarine, and lard. Liquid fats, also known as oils—olive, canola, safflower, peanut, grape-seed, and corn oil—are mostly plant based.

Solid fats are a major source of saturated and trans fatty acids. The USDA reports in the Dietary Guide for Americans: "The body uses some saturated fatty acids for physiological and structural functions, but it makes more than enough to meet those needs. People therefore have no dietary requirement for saturated fatty acids."

A simple way to reduce those unnecessary saturated and trans-fatty acids when cooking at home is by replacing solid fats with liquid oils, such as using olive oil instead of butter.

Alligators and Athletes

The University of Florida is so serious about its sports that it invented a drink to rehydrate its football players.

When athletes sweat, they lose electrolytes. That can lead to dehydration and impede muscle function, so university researchers created an electrolyte-based beverage to replenish the sodium and potassium lost on the field. Purposefully there is no fruit juice, as it can cause intestinal upset when exercising.

Since the University of Florida football team is known as the "Gators," the thirst quencher was named Gator-ade. It could have also been named Gator-aid, since it's beneficial to the athletes, but "ade," a suffix meaning "drink," was chosen.

Are Brown Eggs Healthier Than White Eggs, and What Do Earlobes Have to Do with It?

I've always reached for the brown eggs, because I thought they were healthier. Just like I choose brown bread over the processed white.

Guess what? There is no nutritional difference between brown and white eggs. Hens with white feathers and white earlobes produce white-shelled eggs. Hens with brownish-red feathers and red earlobes produce brown-shelled eggs.

Who knew chickens had earlobes?

Eggs are an eggcellent source of protein. And it's no yolk, the color of the yolk depends on what the hens eat. It's also where the majority of the egg's thirteen essential vitamins and minerals are found.

If Humpty Dumpty Sat on a Wall and He Had a Great Fall, Would His Shell Break?

Are you an edge cracker? Do you make it a point to crack your eggs on the edge of a pan or the counter?

Tsk, tsk! No wonder your shell is in smithereens. It may seem like the most efficient way, but the pros do it differently. They crack their eggs on a flat surface. Strike your egg on the counter or the cutting board. Use your thumbs to gently pry open the shell at the center of the crack.

You won't need Humpty Dumpty's men to put your eggs back together ever again.

Eat-Your-Veggies Frittata

Serves 6

I was with a gaggle of girlfriends in Saratoga when I started making this frittata. Using egg whites saves about 110 calories a serving (yolks, on average, are 55 calories each), but feel free to use whole eggs for a richer result. The only nonnegotiable ingredients are the veggies.

---

1 tablespoon butter

1 tablespoon olive oil

1 cup cottage cheese

2 cups egg whites (or a 16-ounce container liquid egg whites, or 10 to 12 whole eggs, or a half-and-half combination)

¼ cup onion, minced

1 cup zucchini, sliced

½ cup mushrooms, sliced

½ cup tomatoes, chopped

½ teaspoon salt

2 cups packed spinach leaves

✤ Preheat the oven to 350°F.

✤ Whisk the cottage cheese into the egg whites and set aside.

✤ In a 10-inch nonstick or ceramic ovenproof skillet, melt the butter in the olive oil over medium-low heat. Add the onion to the skillet and cook until softened, about 2 to 3 minutes. Add the zucchini and continue to cook 5 minutes. Add the mushrooms and cook until softened, about 2 minutes. Mix in the chopped tomatoes and salt and cook 2 to 3 minutes. Add the spinach and cook until it just wilts, about 2 to 3 minutes.

✤ Rewhisk the egg mixture briefly and pour it into the skillet. Increase the heat to medium. Cook on the stovetop until the eggs are opaque—the outer edges should be set—about 5 minutes.

✤ Put the skillet in the oven. Bake the frittata for 10 to 15 minutes or until the eggs are no longer runny. Remove the pan from the oven and allow the eggs to set for 10 minutes. Serve warm.

Negotiable Ingredients

It's fine to add ½ cup of cooked bacon, chicken, or crumbled sausage if you're missing the meat. If you aren't a calorie or cholesterol crusader, replace the cottage cheese with cheddar or jack.

POSTSCRIPT

The cooked frittata will stay fresh in the refrigerator for two to three days. I have made it on a leisurely Sunday morning and enjoyed the leftovers the following weekday mornings for breakfast.

Egg-cellent Eggs

According to the USDA's Food Safety and Inspection Service, the three grades of eggs, AA, A, and B, are determined by the interior quality of the egg plus the appearance and condition of the eggshell.

B-grade eggs means the yolks will be flatter and the whites thinner than A or AA eggs. We rarely see these eggs in the supermarket, as they are used to make egg products. Hallmarks of the premium AA-grade egg are high and round yolks and whites that are thick and firm. A-grade are similar to their AA counterpart, except that the whites are "reasonably firm."

Consider using A-grade eggs for cracking into mixes and recipes or for scrambling. For poaching and frying, firm AA-grade eggs are recommended and worth the bigger price.

Grading has nothing to do with freshness. Purchase eggs before the sell-by or expiration date stamped on the carton. (The eggs were usually packed thirty days *before* that date.) Store them in their original carton in the coldest part of your refrigerator. The eggs won't suffer significant quality loss for at least three weeks from the time you brought them home, even though the sell-by or expiration date may have passed. Interestingly, they are more likely to dry up than spoil.

There is an egg-ception—if you leave your eggs at room temperature, they'll age more in one day than one week in the refrigerator. (Not to mention the bacteria danger.)

Secrets the Easter Bunny Never Told You

The kids are giddy and ready to dunk eggs into the dye. But first things first. Use older eggs, not fresh eggs.

I know that we instinctively want the freshest of foods, especially for our children, but here's an instance where you want to use eggs that have been in the fridge awhile. The whites of fresh eggs cling tightly to the shell. As the eggs age, the whites release, and that makes peeling the eggshell much easier.

The Easter Bunny may not have told you this, either—hard-boiling is not the preferred cooking method. Turbulent water makes the eggs bump into each other, and that can result in cracked shells. Plus, the high heat can lead to the (harmless) dreaded greenish-gray ring around the yolk, a chemical reaction caused by overcooking.

Here's how I prepare mine. Place eggs in the pan and cover with cool water. Cook them at medium heat until the water starts to boil. Then turn off the heat immediately and cover the pan. After 15 minutes take them off the stove and run cold tap water over the eggs until they are cool enough to handle. The eggs will peel the easiest while they are still warm.

If you want your yolks to be in the center of the egg instead of at the end, take them out of the carton and store them on their sides overnight before cooking them.

The Devil Made Me Do It

Have you ever wondered why we call eggs "deviled"? If they include hot or spicy ingredients, such as curry or Worcestershire sauce, they qualify as deviled.

I can't call my eggs deviled, since I do not use anything spicy, not even mustard. "Stuffed eggs" is the proper term if you prefer your eggs mild like mine.

Yolkey Dokey

Ever the punster, when asked if I will bring stuffed eggs to a picnic or gathering I always answer, "Yolkey dokey."

12 pieces

6 hard-boiled eggs (see "Secrets the Easter Bunny Never Told You," page 252)

¼ cup mayonnaise, Best Foods or Hellmann's preferred

¼ teaspoon celery salt

⅛ teaspoon garlic powder

1 teaspoon minced chives

1 teaspoon lemon juice

Sweet paprika

✛ Peel the eggs and slice them in half.

✛ Remove the yolks. Place in a bowl and mash until fine with a fork.

✛ Mix in the mayonnaise, celery salt, garlic powder, lemon, and chives.

✛ Stuff the eggs with the mixture.

✛ Dust the eggs lightly with sweet paprika.

✛ Chill until ready to serve.

POSTSCRIPT

I don't have a stuffed or deviled egg platter. I can't justify the shelf space for the amount of times I use it in a year. Instead, I create a custom carrier with an egg carton. Snip ¼ inch off the cardboard peaks to create tiny vases. Fill them with parsley sprigs. Line each of the twelve craters with lettuce leaves and place the eggs on top of them. Store the eggs covered in the refrigerator and keep cool while transporting.

What Can Noah's Ark Teach You About Poaching Eggs?

My guests are often impressed with my poached eggs. They say they only eat poached eggs out, because they can't cook them at home. My method is simple and reliable. Before I had success with it, my grandmother was poaching with pride for fifty years.

Start by doing what Noah did: two by two. I have the best luck cooking two at a time, even if I have to make several batches.

Use a small pot that has a lid, not a flat pan. Fill the pot three-quarters full of water and add 1 teaspoon of white vinegar. The vinegar does its magic by helping to bring the eggs back together again. Set the pan on medium-high heat.

Crack both eggs in a small bowl. This will ensure your yolks are not broken and the eggs are shell free, and the bowl makes it easy to slip the eggs into the water.

When the water is boiling, add the eggs. Don't step away! The water will begin to foam shortly, and just as the foam is about to boil over the pot, turn off the heat and cover immediately. Set your alarm for 3 minutes.

Remove the eggs with a slotted spoon, taking extra care to shake off excess water.

Eggs Benedictine

Serves 4

Eggs Benedict with an Italian twist. I replace the Canadian bacon (which really is ham) with Italian ham, aka prosciutto. The hollandaise is swapped for red sauce. Say *arrivederci* to the traditional English muffin. Rustic Italian bread, such as ciabatta, is suggested here.

---

4 slices prosciutto

4 slices provolone cheese

4 slices rustic Italian bread

4 poached eggs

¾ cup prepared red sauce (or my Smooshed Sauce, page 141), heated

✤ Preheat the oven to broil.

✤ Place a slice of prosciutto and then a slice of cheese on each of the bread slices. Place them under broiler until they are melted and brown on edges. Remove them from oven and place on a warm plate.

✤ Poach the eggs, drain them well, and place them on top of the cheese. Season to taste with salt and pepper. Cover each egg with 3 tablespoons of red sauce.

Why Should You Whip Egg Whites in an Operating Room?

I eat egg whites several mornings a week. As a former fatty, I prefer to avoid the calories in the yolks, which average 55 calories each.

When whipping egg whites, say, for an omelet or a meringue, it is critical to be sure that no oil or traces of yolk are in the whites, or on the bowl, or on the whisk.

Any fat, including butter or grease, will thwart your egg-white beating or volumizing efforts.

Anything that touches the egg whites has to be clean—or sterile, just like the instruments in a surgical suite.

Why Do You Need a Bible When Ordering Prosciutto at a Deli?

The Italians take their prosciutto, salt-cured and air-dried ham, very seriously. So much so that they have an expression, "You should be able to read the Bible through a slice of prosciutto."

When ordering prosciutto at a deli, do what the Italians do. Ask to see the first slice before you commit to the order. After you have inspected it to be sure it is cut thin enough, ask to have the slices layered, not stacked.

You'll look like a pro, and you'll be able to read your favorite Bible verse through the transparent ham.

Brad Cola

You've heard about Coca Cola, but how about Brad Cola?

Pepsi-Cola was created in 1898 by pharmacist Caleb Bradham. His customers called it "Brad's Drink," and a few years later it was renamed Pepsi-Cola.

"Cola" comes from one of the key ingredients, the caffeine-containing kola nut, but what about the Pepsi? Perhaps because of the digestive enzyme pepsin? Kind of like Pepto-Bismol? Bradham was a pharmacist, after all . . .

meat

A Chicken May Not Tell You Her Age, but I Will

Farmers use particular terms to identify the age of chickens when they are processed.

Broiler-fryers are about seven weeks old. Roasters are three to five months old. Stewing chickens range between ten and eighteen months old. Age does have an advantage—flavor—but the extra time on the farm can make stewing chickens tough, thus their name, because they are best stewed.

What about those brown age spots? The darkening you sometimes see around the bones after the chicken is cooked? That occurs primarily in broiler-fryers, because they are young and their bones have not hardened completely. The pigment is from the bone marrow "bleeding" through.

How Can the Planet Mars Help You Make a Better Burger?

Of all planets in the solar system that we can observe, Mars has the distinction of having the largest crater. Craters are one of the keys to a great burger.

Starting out with a uniformly flat patty usually results in a burger with breaking and curling edges. Instead, create a shallow crater in the center of your burger, and the patty will flatten as it cooks and shrinks.

Are you a frequent flipper? I thought you were supposed to leave the burger alone and turn only one time, but you'll get a moister burger if you gently flip a few times—your burger won't absorb too much heat on any one side. Not only will your meat cook faster, the turning protects the outer edges (the ones that are now flat thanks to your crater) from overcooking.

Should You Chill with Your Chicken?

You may not want to hang out on the couch sipping a beer with your chicken, but if you like crispy skin, chilling it salted and uncovered is the key. Air-drying poultry in the refrigerator removes moisture from the skin.

Place a rack (it can be like the one you use to cool cookies) on top of a sheet pan. Put the whole chicken on top of the rack and season with salt. Sometimes I add lemon zest. Do not cover the chicken. Place in the refrigerator for several hours or, even better, overnight.

Roasting the bird at a high heat, 375 to 400°F, will ensure that this technique does not run afowl.

Why Can't You Order Sweet and Sour Pork for Sixteen?

Well, you can, although you may need multiple orders. Neighborhood Chinese restaurants cook in quantities of pints and quarts, and that's not because of the size of their containers.

The reason is that only small quantities cook efficiently in the wok. The secret to stir-frying is cooking at high temperatures for a short amount of time. Too much food at one time in a crowded wok will reduce the heat necessary to cook it correctly.

There are exceptions, such as food-court restaurants and buffets. Since they prepare their food in bigger batches, they have extra-large woks and custom-made stoves to accommodate cooking larger quantities.

Pork Tacos with Watermelon Salsa

Serves 6 as a main course or 12 as an appetizer

When Guy Fieri and I were doing our radio program, *The Food Guy and Marcy Show*, Guy often referred to himself as a POP—Pal of Pork. And why not? It's a versatile meat that's full of flavor. This recipe is one of my favorites from the *Guy Fieri Food* cookbook.

SALSA

2 tablespoons rice vinegar

¼ cup olive oil

1½ tablespoons soy sauce

¼ teaspoon sesame oil

1 cup watermelon, cut into ¼-inch cubes

1 cup seeded English cucumber, cut into ¼-inch cubes

1 Hass avocado, pitted, peeled, and cut into ¼-inch cubes

✤ Make the vinaigrette by whisking together the rice vinegar, olive oil, soy sauce, and sesame oil. In a medium bowl, combine the watermelon, cucumber, and avocado and very gently fold in the vinaigrette. Chill.

TACOS

1 pork tenderloin, silverskin removed, cut into 1-inch slices

1 tablespoon onion powder

1 teaspoon red chili pepper flakes

1 teaspoon freshly ground pepper

2 tablespoons fresh ginger, chopped

2 tablespoons garlic, minced

3 tablespoons soy sauce

2 tablespoons oyster sauce

½ teaspoon sesame oil

1 head romaine lettuce

✤ To make the pork, combine all the ingredients except the lettuce in a resealable 1-gallon plastic bag and let marinate for 30 minutes.

✤ Trim off the soft dark green end of the romaine. Cut off the root end and separate the leaves to create six 4-inch-long lettuce "shells" for dinner-size portions. Rinse, dry, and chill the leaves.

✤ Preheat a grill to medium. Discard the marinade. Grill the pork for 3 minutes on each side. Remove it from the heat, let it rest 3 minutes, and roughly chop it into ½ -inch pieces.

✤ Fill the lettuce shells with the pork, top with the salsa, and devour!

Should You Teach Your Steak How to Tell Time?

The answer is yes, if you want mouth-watering grill marks on your steak. I'd always admired the char-burned crisscross lines on steaks at restaurants, but I'd never been able to achieve them at home.

Until I started using the clock to guide me. Now I designate one end of the steak as the top. If there is a fatty end, you can make that the top. However, I find it easier to put a toothpick at one end to make it obvious. After a while, all steaks start looking the same.

Step One: Start with the toothpick facing two o'clock. As soon as there are diagonal grill marks on the bottom side and it is not sticking, go to step two.

Step Two: Rotate the steak, keeping it on the same side, until the toothpick is pointing toward ten o'clock. When there are crisscross grill marks on the bottom side and it lifts easily without sticking, proceed to step three.

Step Three: Flip and turn the steak back to two o'clock. Finish cooking your steak here until it has reached your desired degree of doneness.

Lift with the tongs and place on a warm platter to rest.

Serve the steak with your professional crisscross lines on top. No one is going to peek under the steak and see it has only one diagonal line.

With practice, you'll be a marksman in no time.

Chopped Liver Versus Paté

If it's chopped liver, then it's made of liver and rendered chicken fat, which my cooking pal Bubbie refers to as schmaltz, hard-boiled eggs, and onion.

Chopped liver is just that, chopped, while paté is a mixture known as an emulsion, is smooth and sliced, and includes ingredients such as shallots and brandy. Now you'll be able to say, "What am I? Chopped liver?" and know the answer.

Should You Blow-Dry Your Chicken?

It's not about perfectly coiffed feathers; it's about perfectly crispy skin.

Use your blow dryer on the "no heat" setting to dry your bird. The circulating air will help draw the moisture from the skin, giving your chicken a crispy crust when roasted in a hot, dry oven.

When Is It Okay to Touch Your Food?

When cooking your steak. It can help you determine doneness.

The fleshy part of your hand between your thumb and index finger, can help you determine how far along your steak is when it's cooking.

Make an "okay" sign with your hand. If the fleshy part between your thumb and index finger feels like the steak does when pressed, the steak is rare. If you close your fist, curling your thumb lightly over your index finger, and your steak feels like the web of your hand, it's medium. If you close your fist tightly and that's how the meat feels, it's well done.

As your steak is cooking, touch it several times to see how soft it is compared to the web of your hand. The softer the steak, the rarer it will be. The firmer the steak, the more done it is. It will take practice to trust the process, but it's far preferable to cutting into your steak to see if it's done. That allows the precious juices and flavors to run out, and the result will be a drier steak.

Skirt Steaks and Split Skirts

Yesiree, they are both cuts of beef. One you might recognize and one you might not.

Skirt steak is the long slab you often see folded in the butcher's case that loves a good marinade.

Coulotte is the name for a split skirt that originated in France and also the name for an overlooked, yet delicious, cut of beef from the cap of the sirloin.

Many chefs covet the coulotte's beefy flavor. It's less expensive than filet mignon, yet close in texture. With a coulotte steak you'll save money and calories—it's considered among the leanest cuts of beef.

Greek "Tootsie" Pops

18 pieces

My homage to Tootsie Pops and the irresistible Tootsie Roll center. I'll wager that Mr. Owl would eat them in one bite, not three! Serve with tzatziki sauce for zest and zing.

FOR THE "TOOTSIE" POPS

1 pound ground lamb

¼ cup onion, minced

¼ cup parsley, chopped

2 large cloves garlic, minced

1 tablespoon lemon juice

1 teaspoon salt

¼ teaspoon cumin

Pitted Kalamata olives

4 or 4 ½-inch lollipop sticks (available in the baking section and at culinary stores)

Aluminum foil or parchment paper

FOR THE TZATZIKI SAUCE

1 large cucumber, peeled and seeded

1 cup plain Greek yogurt

1 teaspoon dill, minced

1 garlic clove, minced

1 tablespoon lemon juice

1 teaspoon salt

FOR THE "TOOTSIE" POPS

✤ Preheat the oven to 350°F.

✤ In a large bowl, combine the first seven ingredients. Mix well.

✤ Place one olive at the end of a lollipop stick. Using the lamb mixture, make a flat half dollar in your hand and wrap around the olive. Finished, it should be a bit bigger than a regular Tootsie Pop to allow for shrinkage when baking.

✤ Place pops on a sheet pan lined with foil or parchment.

✤ Bake 20 minutes or until cooked through. Drain on paper towels.

FOR THE TZATZIKI SAUCE

✤ Grate the cucumber. Take care to squeeze all the excess water out. Place the cucumber in the mixing bowl.

✤ Add the other five ingredients and put in the refrigerator.

✤ Serve chilled in a bowl surrounded by warm Greek "Tootsie" Pops.

Did Your Chicken Get a Good Workout?

How much a chicken exercises explains why the legs are dark and the breast meat is white.

Myoglobin is the red or purple protein that delivers oxygen to the muscles and determines the pigment of the flesh. The more an animal exercises, the more muscle it uses, and the more myoglobin it needs.

The chicken's breast is white because, other than being used to flutter the wings occasionally, those muscles are relatively inactive. Since the chicken legs are doing the standing and walking, those muscles need more myoglobin; hence the darker pigment.

Chex Mix Chicken on a Stick

Serves 6

Aunt Sally is the type of woman who attends every Winn Dixie opening within two hundred miles of her Winter Park, Florida, home. She's whacky, lovable, and very Southern. When my son was two, Sally showed me how to wrap the ends of the drumstick. Taking the kid-friendly feature further, I use Chex Mix to coat the chicken. The kids love the handle and moms love the clean hands.

1½ cups Chex Mix

1 teaspoon salt

Paprika, garlic powder, cayenne, pepper as desired

6 chicken drumsticks

Vegetable oil for frying

✤ Preheat the oven to 375°F.

✤ Place the Chex Mix in a food processor and pulse it until pulverized. Place the crumbs on large plate. Add salt and seasonings to taste, depending on how adventurous your kids are. Dredge the chicken in the mixture.

✤ Place enough oil in a pan to cover the bottom and heat on medium-high for 3 to 4 minutes. Gently fry drumsticks, three at a time, about 2 minutes on a side or just enough to achieve a crispy crust. Transfer the drumsticks to a foil-lined sheet pan and bake for 30 minutes.

✤ Take the chicken off the sheet pan and let the drumsticks cool on a wire rack for 10 minutes. Wrap the ends of the drumsticks several times with pieces of paper towel and secure with rubber bands.

Why Does the Butcher Need an Anatomy Class?

There is nothing better than slow-roasted pork butt, the makings of crispy carnitas and pulled-pork sandwiches.

Recipes like these often call for a pork butt, also called Boston butt, the fatty and flavorful part of the pig. Except it is not the gluteus maximus of the pig you're eating; it's the front shoulder.

Wouldn't you think the butcher who coined the cut would know the difference between the rear end of the pig and the shoulder? Why the anatomically incorrect name? Why Boston?

I e-mailed my pal Bruce Aidells, author of *The Complete Book of Pork*, for the answers. He explained that "butt" is the name of the barrel used in Boston to ship the lesser cuts of the pig, including the shoulder, during Colonial times. It has nothing to do with the rear end of a pig.

Test-Tube Taco Meat

The future is here—and it's test-tube meat. Scientists are growing meat in the lab, starting with only a few stem cells from a cow.

Growing in-vitro meat is similar to the technique scientists use to grow human cells and tissues. They aren't creating meat on the bone (that's too intricate), but they can grow ground meats such as beef, pork, and chicken.

I am not a fan of Frankenfoods; however, it is compelling that with this scientific technique no animals are slaughtered, it's sustainable, and it could help feed the millions of people on our planet who are hungry.

Are you asking yourself if you would eat test-tube hamburger meat? Well, I have to admit that I wouldn't do it voluntarily, but I'm bold enough to bet that as long as there was a familiar flavor and texture, I wouldn't be able to tell the difference in a blind taste test.

MEAT

The Raw Truth

My grandmother made chicken five days a week, and she always rinsed it. I can still see her leaning over the sink to get the chicken nice and clean.

I've done the same thing since I was fourteen years old. So imagine my surprise when I saw my pal Guy Fieri on *Guy's Big Bite,* opening a package of chicken, ripping off the cellophane, and throwing the chicken directly into the frying pan. Ewwww!

I was so worried that he made a serious gaffe on national television that I went to the USDA's website to get him the safety information. I ruffled my own feathers when I read the answer: "Washing raw poultry before cooking it is not recommended. Bacteria in raw meat and poultry juices can be spread to other foods, utensils, and surfaces. This is called cross-contamination. Rinsing or soaking chicken does not destroy bacteria. Any bacteria that might be present on fresh chicken are destroyed only by cooking."

I confess that whenever I challenged Guy on our show, it was because I thought I was right. In the case of rinsing chicken before cooking it, I was wrong, and despite the evidence, I still do it. (Fear not—I sanitize counters and cutting boards.)

It Boils Down to This

When I was in my twenties, my "secret" for ribs was boiling them in beer. I thought I was getting my ribs moist before baking or grilling them. I've since learned that all I did was strip my ribs of fat and flavor, with all their juiciness lost in the cloudy beer I threw away.

Slow and low cooking is my preferred method today, plus there is one more thing I do to ensure my ribs are as tender as they can be.

Ribs have a tough membrane on their underside sometimes referred to as the silverskin. In order to have fall-off-the-bone ribs, the membrane must be removed before cooking, regardless of the technique you are using. Slip your finger under the membrane along the last rib bone and gently pull the membrane away. When I make ribs for a crowd, I preorder them from my butcher with the silverskin removed.

Rest Test

What is it about a perfectly seared steak coming off the grill that compels us to eat it immediately? We know it needs to rest, which allows the juices to redistribute evenly throughout the meat, but sometimes waiting is unbearable.

I confess that I used to serve my meat "while it was hot," but after an Art and Science of Cooking class at the Culinary Institute of America, I've seen how patience is rewarded.

In a controlled kitchen study, we took two identical steaks and cooked them to the same internal temperature. The first steak was allowed to rest. The second steak was sliced immediately.

Ten minutes later we did the evaluation. The rested steak had very little blood on the plate. When we cut into it, no juices leaked out. It was tender and medium rare. The steak that had been cut right after it was finished cooking, on the other hand, was lying in a pool of blood. Its texture was tougher and the taste less flavorful.

Rest assured, good meat comes to those who wait.

Keeping Abreast of Your Chicken

Chickens have one anatomical breast, not two. Their one breast wraps around their chest like a coat of armor on a knight.

When the breast is halved, it becomes two pieces. We are familiar with the split breast, because butchers split the chicken breast into two pieces prior to sale and label it as such.

Why Is There an Oyster in Your Chicken?

I rarely debone my own chicken, but I just might start, if only for the oyster.

No, not the briny bivalve. I'm referring to the sweet morsel of meat that is attached to the backbone. The French refer to this poultry prize as *sot-l'y-laisse,* which loosely translates as "the part only a fool leaves behind."

I guess I've been a fool for years, because I didn't know it existed until I watched Chef John DeShetler, Culinary Institute of America professor, demonstrate how to debone a chicken.

In a whole chicken, you can identify the oysters by the little bumps under the skin, over the thighs, and next to the backbone. Removing them is trickier, but with practice and knowing how to locate them, you'll find the joint and be able to pop them out with a sharp boning knife.

For those less inclined to search for buried treasure with a sharp knife, beg your butcher for them or be on the lookout for chicken oysters, or *sot-l'y-laisse,* on fine restaurant menus.

Trains Have Conductors and So Does Prime Rib

I started calling myself a homecooker on *The Food Guy and Marcy Show.* (It distinguished me from our expert guests.) It means that I am a step above the average home cook and several notches below a gourmet cook. I know to take out the meat 10 degrees below the desired degree of doneness. Yet I confess I have overcooked my prime rib more than a few times, despite pulling it out early.

Recently, a theory was introduced to me: while the beef was resting, the bones were still hot, acting as heat conductors, and they raised the internal temperature even higher.

Although there are many variables, consider removing meat with bones from the oven just a bit sooner than you would a boneless cut.

✤

acknowledgments

Applause goes to:

My grandparents, Vera and Arthur, whom I nicknamed Germy and Fa, for providing the love and stability in my childhood that gave me the courage to be the person I am today. Their love of words and dictionaries are their legacy with me.

Aunt Holly, our family's historian, for remembering all the details I never knew or have forgotten, and for being my trusted reader. My mom, Judy, whose lack of interest in the kitchen fueled mine.

Tom, Bo, and Riley Rose, for the latitude and love to reinvent myself.

There can be too many cooks in the kitchen, but when it comes to editing a book, there can never be enough editors or partners in print. First and foremost, Nancy Hancock, for jumping into the fry pan with *SNACKS*, for all the giggles and guidance, and for her confidence in me before I had confidence in myself. Your "Hancock with a hammer" style has made me a better writer.

Elsa Dixon, for her calm cadence, encouragement, and fierce loyalty to grammar. My team at HarperCollins, including Suzanne Quist, Michele Wetherbee, Terri Leonard, and the entire dedicated book brigade in production, publicity, and promotion.

Sheryl Chapman, for the vibrant and creative illustrations that tell the stories better than words alone.

Charles Dubin, for inviting me on the set for the final season of *M*A*S*H* and for helping me realize that I really didn't want to direct. Ken Kragen, the mentor with the mostest. Brian Hudson, for the call and coaching that led to my becoming a radio host. Deana Kodiak, for producing *The Marcy Smothers Show* and *The Food Guy and Marcy Show*. If there was ever a person who had my back, it was you. Peter Ciccarelli, for his unwavering support and encouragement over the years. Rick Eytcheson, for the suggestion I create and produce a national food, wine, and lifestyle radio show and for the introduction to KFBK. Jeff Holden, Alan Eisensen, and Mike Murray of KFBK in Sacramento, for being the first station to carry *The Food Guy and Marcy Show,* and to all the affiliates across the country who followed after that. Jack Levar, for his counsel early in the process. Mike McVay and Holland Cooke, consultants extraordinaire, who helped me take

The Food Guy and Marcy Show to levels I never could have achieved on my own. KWAV's Kathy Baker and Rick Buckley, of the WOR Network, for the meeting I was stunned to get and for the excellent feedback on my radio SNACKS. KZST, for carrying *The Food Guy and Marcy Show* in Sonoma County, plus Jacqui Bailey, for the editing, and Eric Peter, for the early morning satellite rescues. (And Deb, because she'll kill me for not mentioning her.) George Buce, Randy Wells, Eric LeMessurier, and Ben "Tiny" Hawk, for the engineering expertise. Chef Justin Wangler and the Kendall-Jackson Wine Center, for providing the venue to record our show and the sit-down lunches that Guy and I, our crew, and guests adored.

And with my deepest appreciation, Brent Farris, for the original radio feature concept that led to this book, plus the support, time in the studio, and mentorship that made it all possible.

Guy Fieri, for his loyalty and dedication to our show, for suggesting that I start taking classes at the Culinary Institute of America, and for believing in me from day one. John Lasseter, for being the first person to insist that I write this book, and his wife, Nancy, both the best friends ever. Mollie Katzen, for the encouragement to proceed and for the introduction to my agent, Steve Troha at Folio Literary Management. Steve—thanks for everything, including resuscitating this project and nagging me to find a better way to organize the book, and for bringing *SNACKS* to Nancy, one of your favorite editors.

My advisers, teachers, supporters, and cooking cohorts: Chef Mark Ainsworth and Chef John DeShetler, at the Culinary Institute of America in Hyde Park. Wine Master Richard Arrowood, for generously sharing his enology expertise. Bruce Aidells, for always answering my beef and pork e-mail queries. Clark Wolf, the voice of reason and all things cheese. Arnie Riebli, fourth-generation egg farmer, for his patience with me, even though it doesn't come naturally to him. Kurt Ramsey at K.T.'s kitchen, for the Green Goddess dressing research. Jack Daniel's Master Distiller Jeff Arnett, for all things whiskey. Chef Takeshi Uchida, for the sushi and advice about Japanese cuisine. Chef Lisa Hemenway, for feeding me well at Fresh as I wrote these pages. Vince Albano and Mary's Pizza Shack, for the pizza-box recycling investigation. Matthew Lowe, Kendall-Jackson's garden gnome. Alexander Kiernan, for the sage and timely advice. Terry "Crab Man" Cosgrove. Spiritual adviser Steve Beal. Lynne Olver of Foodtimeline.org, and Chef James of Foodreference.com. Jodie Lau and G & G Market in Petaluma. Also from the Culinary Institute of America, Chef Corky Clark and Jay Blotcher, plus fellow students Mark, Linda, the Three Amigos, and Wounded Warrior Mark from Boston. Chef Mary Bergin, for the Sur La Table cooking classes. Charlene Rouspil at Dacor, for the cookware. Barbara Banke and Peggy Furth, for their thrill when I "got an order." Sid Bloom, for being my valued "man on the street" taster, and his wife, Maxine, aka Bubbie, for testing all the recipes and lending her experience, expertise, and humor.

My final expression of gratitude is for an unlikely lucky charm.

When I exited the parking garage at One Embarcadero in San Francisco following my initial meeting and interview with Nancy Hancock at HarperOne, the elderly attendant asked me how my day in the city had been.

"Good." I was still reeling. "I think I may have sold a book."

Confused, he responded, "What book did you buy?"

"I didn't buy a book. I met an editor about publishing my book." I was hoping I wasn't jinxing myself.

"Well, then, congratulations. I'd like an autographed copy. My name is Arthur. Don't forget."

"I won't forget. My grandfather's name was Arthur." I paid the fee and left.

The offer for *SNACKS* came from HarperOne one week later. It was four years after I recorded my first SNACK for *The Food Guy and Marcy Show*. I hadn't jinxed myself after all.

Arthur, I remembered, and the first copy of my book is for you.

foodography

The following books were invaluable resources that I consulted frequently:

Davidson, Alan. *The Oxford Companion to Food.* Oxford: Oxford Univ. Press, 1999.

Herbst, Sharon Tyler. *The Food Lover's Companion.* New York: Barron's Educational Series, 2001.

McGee, Harold. *On Food and Cooking: The Science and Lore of the Kitchen.* New York: Scribner, 1984.

The Culinary Institute of America. *The Professional Chef,* 9th ed. Hoboken, NJ: Wiley, 2011.

REFERENCE BOOKS

Aidells, Bruce, with Lisa Weiss. *Bruce Aidells's Complete Book of Pork: A Guide to Buying, Storing, and Cooking the World's Favorite Meat.* New York: HarperCollins, 2004.

Berolzheimer, Ruth, ed. *500 Snacks and Bright Ideas for Entertaining.* Chicago: Consolidated, 1940.

Child, Julia. *From Julia Child's Kitchen.* New York: Gramercy Books, 1970.

Cox, Jeff. *The Organic Food Shopper's Guide.* Hoboken, NJ: Wiley, 2008.

Hazan, Marcella. *Essentials of Classic Italian Cooking.* New York: Knopf, 1993.

Herbst, Sharon Tyler, and Ron Herbst. *The Cheese Lover's Companion.* New York: HarperCollins, 2007.

Mariani, John. *American Food and Drink.* New York: Lebhar-Friedman Books, 1999.

Nestle, Marion. *What To Eat.* New York: North Point, 2006.

Radke, Nancy. *The Seasons of Parmigiano-Reggiano.* Reggio Emilia, Italy: Consorzio del Formaggio Parmigiano-Reggiano, 1998.

Simmons, Marie. *Fig Heaven.* New York: HarperCollins, 2004.

Spieler, Marlena. *Grilled Cheese: Fifty Recipes to Make You Melt.* San Francisco: Chronicle, 2004.

Tarantino, Jim. *Marinades, Rubs, Brines, Cures, and Glazes.* Berkeley, CA: Ten Speed, 2006.

Wakefield, Ruth Graves. *Toll House Tried and True Recipes.* New York: Barrows, 1949.

Wansink, Brian. *Mindless Eating.* New York: Bantam Dell, 2006.

Wolf, Clark. *American Cheeses: The Best Regional, Artisan, and Farmhouse Cheeses, Who Makes Them, and Where to Find Them.* New York: Simon & Schuster, 2008.

Yan, Martin. *Chinatown Cooking.* New York: Morrow, 2002.

"Antioxidant Spices Reduce Negative Effects of High-Fat Meals." *Live,* Penn State University, August 10, 2011. http://live.psu.edu/story/54471.

Baldock, Maurita. "The Eskimo Pie Corporation Records, 1921–1996 #553." Smithsonian National Museum of American History, 1998. http://americanhistory.si.edu/archives/d8553.htm.

Bardin, Jon. "Why Supermarket Tomatoes Tend to Taste Bland." *Los Angeles Times,* June 30, 2012. http://articles.latimes.com/2012/jun/30/science/la-sci-tomato-taste-20120630.

Bewley, Lindsey. "The HemCon Bandage Is a Veritable Shrimp Gumbo, Used to Control Severe Hemorrhagic Bleeding." *Scienceline,* February 26, 2007. http://scienceline.org/2007/02/ask-bewley-shrimpcocktail.

"Dairy Fun Facts and Trivia." University of Illinois Extension. http://my.extension.uiuc.edu.

Harmon, John. "Potato Chips." *Atlas of Popular Culture in the Northeastern United States.* http://www.geography.ccsu.edu/harmonj/atlas/potchips.htm.

Kruglinski, Susan. "The Man Who Found Quarks and Made Sense of the Universe." *Discovery Magazine,* March 17, 2009. http://discovermagazine.com/2009/apr/17-man-who-found-quarks-made-sense-of-universe.

McGee, Harold. "The Curious Cook: On Food and Zapping." *New York Times,* April 2, 2008. http://www.nytimes.com/2008/04/02/dining/02curious.html?_r=1.

———. "The Curious Cook: Prolonging the Life of Berries." *New York Times,* August 26, 2009. http://www.nytimes.com/2009/08/26/dining/26curi.html.

Michaels, Daniels. "Test Flight: Lufthansa Searches for Savor in the Sky." *Wall Street Journal,* July 27, 2010. http://www.wsj.com/article/SB10001424052748703294904575384954227906006.html.

"NCAA Banned Drug List." National Collegiate Athletic Association. http://www.ncaa.org/wps/wcm/connect/public/NCAA/Health+and+Safety/Drug+Testing/Resources/NCAA+banned+drugs+list.

Nestle, Marion. "Untreated Tuna Scrape May Make Sushi Risky Fare." *San Francisco Chronicle,* May 4, 2012. http://www.sfgate.com/food/article/Untreated-tuna-scrape-may-make-sushi-risky-fare–3535539.php.

Reichl, Ruth. "Ruth Reichl Feasts at Mission Chinese Food, Reveals Her Favorite Burrito in L.A." *Grub Street, San Francisco,* January 19, 2012. http://sanfrancisco.grubstreet.com/2012/01/where-ruth-reichl-eats-in-sf-ny-la.html.

Sohn, Emily. "Supermarket Lights Supercharge Vegetables' Nutrition Value." *Discovery News,* March 10, 2010. http://news.discovery.com/earth/supermarkets-vegetables-produce.html.

"Sound Can Change Our Perception of Food." Unilever Global. http://www.unilever.com/innovation/researchdiscoveries/sound.

Strecker, Michael. "Chocolate Toothpaste Better Than Fluoride, Researcher Says." Tulane University, May 16, 2007. http://tulane.edu/news/releases/archive/2007/051607.cfm.

Weise, Elizabeth. "Digging the Baby Carrot." *USA Today,* August 11, 2004. http://www.usatoday.com/life/lifestyle/2004–08–11-baby-carrot_x.htm.

NEWSPAPER AND MAGAZINE ARTICLES

"Frank Dorsa: Inventor of Frozen Waffle." *Seattle Times,* May 18, 2012. Obituary.

Gold, Amanda. "The Breadmaker's Guru." *San Francisco Chronicle,* September 24, 2008. Section F, 1.

Goldman, Russell. "Where's the Beef?," *Vassar Quarterly* (Fall 2011): 26–28.

Mouawad, Jad. "Beyond Mile-High Grub: Can Airline Food Be Tasty?," *New York Times,* March 11, 2012, Sunday Business, 1.

WEBSITES

http://www.auntjemima.com

http://www.avocadocentral.com

http://www.birdseye.com

http://brands.nabisco.com/HoneyMaid/pages/our-history.aspx

http://www.californiafigs.com

http://www.chefboyardee.com

http://www.christopherranch.com

http://www.derbymuseum.org

http://disney.go.com/disneyinsider/history/legends/paul-frees

http://www.dressings-sauces.org/mayonnaise.html

http://www.drpeppermuseum.com

http://duncanhines.com/about-us

http://www.endive.com

http://www.freshcaliforniagrapes.com

http://www.fsis.usda.gov

http://www.fsis.usda.gov/Factsheets/Chicken_from_Farm_To_Table/index.asp

http://www.fsis.usda.gov/Factsheets/Focus_On_Shell_Eggs/index.asp

http://www.gatorade.com/frequently_asked_questions

http://www.glycemicindex.com

http://www.gma.org/lobsters/trivia.html

http://heinzketchup.com

http://www.heinz.com/our-food/products/oreida.aspx

http://www.incredibleegg.org

http://www.jackdaniels.com

http://www.kraft.com/Brands/largest-brands/brands-A/a1.html

http://www.leggomyeggo.com

http://www.livestockexpo.org

http://www.livestrong.com/article/487995-does-mustard-burn-fat

http://www.mars.com/global/brands/chocolate.aspx

http://www.mayoclinic.com/health/caffeine/AN01211

http://www.michelob.com/AppreciatingPouringBeer.aspx

http://www.montereybayaquarium.org/cr/seafoodwatch.aspx

http://www.mrscubbisons.com

http://www.mrspauls.com

http://www.nissinfoods.com

http://www.oceanmist.com

http://www.oreida.com/products/or-tater-tots.aspx

http://www.oreo.eu/oreo/page?siteid=oreo-prd&locale=uken1&PagecRef=620

http://www.pepsico.com

http://www.phillips.com

http://www.popcorn.org

http://www.popsicle.com

http://www.potatogoodness.com

http://www.pringles.com

http://www.robertmondavi.com/history

http://www.scientificamerican.com/article.cfm?id=raw-veggies-are-healthier

http://www.sfpalace.com/garden-court

http://snacks.kraftfoodscompany.com/home/index.aspx

http://www.snopes.com/food/prepare/breadtag.asp

http://www.sutterhome.com/about_history.php

http://www.tabasco.com

http://www.teausa.com

http://www.thenibble.com/reviews/main/cereals/waffle-history2.asp

http://www.thomasbreads.com

http://www.tootsie.com

http://www.ttb.gov/spirits/faq.shtml

http://www.wholefoodsmarket.com/about-our-products/food-safety/methylmercury-seafood

recipe index by aisle

recipe index by category